TRANSGRESSIONS: CULTUR/
Volume 65

MW00354218

Series Editor:
   Shirley R. Steinberg, *McGill University, Canada*

Founding Editor:
   Joe L. Kincheloe (1950–2008) *The Paulo and Nita Freire International Project for Critical Pedagogy*

Editorial Board
   Jon Austin, *University of Southern Queensland, Australia*
   Norman Denzin, *University of Illinois, Champaign-Urbana, USA*
   Rhonda Hammer, *University of California Los Angeles, USA*
   Nikos Metallinos, *Concordia University, Canada*
   Christine Quail, *McMaster University, Canada*
   Ki Wan Sung, *Kyung Hee University, Seoul, Korea*

This book series is dedicated to the radical love and actions of Paulo Freire, Jesus "Pato" Gomez, and Joe L. Kincheloe.

TRANSGRESSIONS: CULTURAL STUDIES AND EDUCATION

Cultural studies provides an analytical toolbox for both making sense of educational practice and extending the insights of educational professionals into their labors. In this context *Transgressions: Cultural Studies and Education* provides a collection of books in the domain that specify this assertion. Crafted for an audience of teachers, teacher educators, scholars and students of cultural studies and others interested in cultural studies and pedagogy, the series documents both the possibilities of and the controversies surrounding the intersection of cultural studies and education. The editors and the authors of this series do not assume that the interaction of cultural studies and education devalues other types of knowledge and analytical forms. Rather the intersection of these knowledge disciplines offers a rejuvenating, optimistic, and positive perspective on education and educational institutions. Some might describe its contribution as democratic, emancipatory, and transformative. The editors and authors maintain that cultural studies helps free educators from sterile, monolithic analyses that have for too long undermined efforts to think of educational practices by providing other words, new languages, and fresh metaphors. Operating in an interdisciplinary cosmos, Transgressions: Cultural Studies and Education is dedicated to exploring the ways cultural studies enhances the study and practice of education. With this in mind the series focuses in a non-exclusive way on popular culture as well as other dimensions of cultural studies including social theory, social justice and positionality, cultural dimensions of technological innovation, new media and media literacy, new forms of oppression emerging in an electronic hyperreality, and postcolonial global concerns. With these concerns in mind cultural studies scholars often argue that the realm of popular culture is the most powerful educational force in contemporary culture. Indeed, in the twenty-first century this pedagogical dynamic is sweeping through the entire world. Educators, they believe, must understand these emerging realities in order to gain an important voice in the pedagogical conversation.

Without an understanding of cultural pedagogy's (education that takes place outside of formal schooling) role in the shaping of individual identity–youth identity in particular–the role educators play in the lives of their students will continue to fade. Why do so many of our students feel that life is incomprehensible and devoid of meaning? What does it mean, teachers wonder, when young people are unable to describe their moods, their affective affiliation to the society around them. Meanings provided young people by mainstream institutions often do little to help them deal with their affective complexity, their difficulty negotiating the rift between meaning and affect. School knowledge and educational expectations seem as anachronistic as a ditto machine, not that learning ways of rational thought and making sense of the world are unimportant.

But school knowledge and educational expectations often have little to offer students about making sense of the way they feel, the way their affective lives are shaped. In no way do we argue that analysis of the production of youth in an electronic mediated world demands some "touchy-feely" educational superficiality. What is needed in this context is a rigorous analysis of the interrelationship between pedagogy, popular culture, meaning making, and youth subjectivity. In an era marked by youth depression, violence, and suicide such insights become extremely important, even life saving. Pessimism about the future is the common sense of many contemporary youth with its concomitant feeling that no one can make a difference.

If affective production can be shaped to reflect these perspectives, then it can be reshaped to lay the groundwork for optimism, passionate commitment, and transformative educational and political activity. In these ways cultural studies adds a dimension to the work of education unfilled by any other sub-discipline. This is what Transgressions: Cultural Studies and Education seeks to produce—literature on these issues that makes a difference. It seeks to publish studies that help those who work with young people, those individuals involved in the disciplines that study children and youth, and young people themselves improve their lives in these bizarre times.

Diversity, Equity, and Inclusive Education

A Voice from the Margins

C.P. Gause
University of North Carolina at Greensboro

SENSE PUBLISHERS
ROTTERDAM/BOSTON/TAIPEI

A C.I.P. record for this book is available from the Library of Congress.

ISBN: 978-94-6091-422-5 (paperback)
ISBN: 978-94-6091-423-2 (hardback)
ISBN: 978-94-6091-424-9 (e-book)

Published by: Sense Publishers,
P.O. Box 21858,
3001 AW Rotterdam,
The Netherlands
https://www.sensepublishers.com

Printed on acid-free paper

DEDICATION

I dedicate this book to my partner and confidant, T. L. H. Your commitment and unwavering support continues to inspire me to engage this work. I love you. Thank you for being a source of strength and inspiration. To our "kids" Bach (Standard Poodle) and Chanel (Miniature Pinscher), thank you so much for the licks, barks, and wagging tails. The both of you continue to remind us of our hope for humanity.

I dedicate this book to the memory of my mother, Ernestine Laverne Lewis-Gause. It has now been 30 years since our God called you home. Not a day has gone by that I have not felt your presence in my life. Your last words continue to inspire me to strive to make a difference on this earth. Thank you for giving me the gift of life.

TABLE OF CONTENTS

PREFACE

In today's society, particularly within the United States, we find ourselves bombarded on a 24-hour daily basis with mediated imagery and sounds that shape our values, belief systems, and moral structures. All social institutions and organizations of our society are impacted by this continuous "streaming cloud." Even those institutions engrossed in their own "traditions"–legal, religious, and political communities– are "infected." The constant bombardment of popular culture on our daily existence informs our identities whether we desire it or not. Due to technological advances, popular culture, broadly defined, encompasses print, digital, virtual, and enhanced mediated imagery that is delivered via "tech" devices (e.g., Blackberry, IPods, Digital phones, HDTV, and hand-held computers) on a 24-hour basis. It consists of chat rooms, virtual text, scripted and unscripted reality TV, music videos, websites, blogs, tweeting, facebooking, and non-stop virtual interaction. Throughout all of this, public education continues to lag behind students' use of technology and popular culture as forms of knowledge production and knowledge consumption. Humanity is connected globally: The best evidence of this fact was the near collapse of world economies generated by the "financial manipulative devices" that I like to call FMDs that were developed by Wall Street firms and other global financial institutions. Fragmented educational institutions, including public schooling and state universities, are often slow in keeping up with what is popular. The lack of a seamless PreK-20 educational system, particularly in the United States, further exacerbates this problem. My key question for this volume is: How has the terrain within the public educational arena evolved from the "sea of possibility" to become the resistant "background noise" of popular culture? We know the meaning and purpose of schooling is being redefined. The relationship between teachers and students, particularly at the secondary level in high schools around the country, has entered into a critical stage of renegotiating what and whose knowledge is of greater value because of a mediated culture (popular culture). Couple this with the corporatization and privatization of public education; no wonder there is a crisis in how knowledge is constructed and produced within this country.

> Publicity turns consumption into a substitute for democracy. The choice of what one eats (or wears or drives) takes the place of significant political choice. Publicity helps to mask and compensate for all that is undemocratic within society. And it also masks what is happening in the rest of the world. (Berger, 1977, p. 149)

To teach, learn, and lead democratically requires the individual to engage in problem posing and in critiquing taken-for-granted narratives of power and privilege. Critical change occurs with significant self-sacrifice, potential alienation/rejection, and costly consequences. Educators must do justice to the larger social, public, and institutional responsibility of our positions, and we must exercise courage in creating opportunities for change.

ACKNOWLEDGEMENTS

This book could not have been completed without the help and assistance of so many great colleagues, scholars, and friends. Many thanks to the following individuals and collective groups for your service and commitment to Inclusive Education: Professor Susan Dennison of The University of North Carolina at Greensboro, Dr. Shirley Steinberg of McGill University; Dr. Dennis Carlson of Miami University; Dr. Donyell Roseboro of The University of North Carolina-Wilmington; Dr. Jean Rosales of The University of North Carolina at Greensboro; Dr. Sam Miller of The University of North Carolina at Greensboro, The Chancellor's Advisory Committee on Equity, Diversity, and Inclusion; The Department of Teacher Education and Higher Education-The University of North Carolina at Greensboro; Ron & Lisa Estes of The Summit Station Eatery-Downtown Greensboro; The Editorial Review and Advisory Boards of The Journal of Black Masculinity; Dr. Tara Green and The African American Studies Program-The University of North Carolina at Greensboro; Professor Duane Cyrus; Mr. Aubrey Lynch; Dr. Michael Dantley of Miami University; Michel Lokhorst of Sense Publishers; The Gause Family, and my students who continue to challenge me epistemologically and ideologically.

INTRODUCTION

When I decided to approach this project, the thing most apparent to me was fear. Fear is a crippling state of being. It operates from the individual's perspective of wanting no surprises and the desire to be aware of every move, position, and thought. I developed an acrostic for the word FEAR: Forever Entrapped And Robbed. The United States is more ideologically, philosophically, culturally, linguistically, racially, and ethnically diverse than she has been in any given point in her history; however, many of her citizens are currently living in a state of fear. I do understand the reasons: the terrorist attacks of September 11, 2001; our government's response to Hurricane Katrina on August 29, 2005; the global economic crisis of 2008–2009; the election of our nations' first African American president; the Gulf Oil Spill; and Arizona immigration legislation of 2010. Many of these events would create such fear; however, all of them have one thing in common: the power and speed with which those events were communicated, broadcast, and streamed across digital airwaves all over the world. What stands out the most is how we allow this fear to take over our lives in multiple ways. We fear our neighbors; therefore, we do not engage them. We fear young people and the way they look; therefore, we do not have conversations with them. We fear the possibility of terrorists' attacks; therefore, we utilize eavesdropping and surveillance devices on our citizens. There are some of us who fear the lost of gun rights; therefore, we stockpile weapons. We fear anything that is different from who we are and what we believe. This nation has, at many points within our history, become more united because of our fear; however, as our borders, physical and virtual, become less protective and the opportunities to connect more via the digital world expand, we must educate our citizenry to not live in fear but in hope.

ONE NATION, ONE WORLD: THE RISE OF A GLOBAL COMMUNITY

Over the past forty years, scholars have engaged the question of how best to educate the nations' citizenry regarding diversity, equity, and inclusion. Banks (1973, 1996, 1997, 2001), Banks-McGhee (1995, 2001), Gay (2000), and Ladson-Billings (1997, 2001, 2005) have researched practices for teachers and educators to better engage in multicultural education and culturally responsive teaching. Teachers and scholars Freire (1970), Kincheloe (1991), and Steinberg (2009) have furthered the discourse through (re)framing how best to educate our students through the framework of critical pedagogy and diversity. Scholars Villaverede and Rodriguez (2000) have interrogated "whiteness" and "white-privilege" as a means of moving educators to critique their own identities. Collaborative activist and scholar Gause (2009) has critiqued Black masculinity and popular culture in order to provide educators and teachers with tools and frameworks for utilizing hip hop and popular culture as mechanisms for creating innovative curriculum.

Individuals and collective communities are influenced by immigration as well as digital migration. The public launch of Google, YouTube, Facebook, and other social networking websites has created opportunities for individuals to engage in 24-hour global sharing, engagement, and interaction via the Internet. The World Wide Web has forever changed the way in which human beings interact with one another and our environment. This has become the essence of globalization. Globalization is the growing expansion and acceleration of the breadth and depth of impact on trans-continental flows and patterns of social interaction across the globe. This process involves the transformation of human organizations by linking communities one to the other without consideration of geographical location.

Although globalization and internationalization are often used interchangeably, they are different. Internationalization is the outcome of economic, social, cultural, and educational globalization. One very visible outcome of this phenomenon is "free trade." Goods that were produced from raw material in one country, manufactured in another country, and transported to another country for citizen consumption are increasingly available. The movement of production and capital, the standardization of consumer tastes, and the legitimization of global capitalism have forever linked all world economies and markets, one outcome of which we witnessed with the great economic world crises of 2008 and 2009. Travelling over the past 25 years, working in educational and non-traditional learning communities across the United States and abroad, has provided me with first-hand opportunities to witness the effects and impact of transnational corporations and globalization. These experiences continue to shape my leadership and teaching philosophy extensively, particularly within the realm of diversity, equity, and inclusive education. On many of those journeys, I have listened to a variety of educators debate the "purpose and process of schooling, within a pluralistic society." Although America is a young nation in comparison with others across the globe, we continue to attract many individuals from foreign lands who seek better lives, political asylum, fame, fortune, and/or to fulfill their dreams. These members of our global humanity bring their distinctive cultures and values, uniquely shaping our 50-state nation. Freire (1970, 1998), Giroux (1995), Carlson (1998), Steinberg & Kincheloe (1991), as cited in Gause (2001), assert

> Culture refers to a system of symbols; more specifically, it is "an historically transmitted pattern of meaning embodied in symbols, a system of inherited conceptions expressed in symbolic form by means of which [humans] communicate, perpetuate and develop their knowledge about and attitudes towards life" …Ritual is a key facet of cultural production…Rituals are 'forms of enacted meaning' which enable "social actors to frame, negotiate, and articulate their…existence as social, cultural, and moral beings" …Rituals, in other words, are components of ideology, helping shape our perceptions of daily life and how we live it. (p. 48)

Culture is socially constructed and lived experiences translated from the meaning making of individuals; that is, how individuals view themselves daily as participants in the world around them and how they make sense of those daily interactions. Culture is not always observable. Culture may be understood through indirect experiences and interactions with self and others, which often require interpretation. Culture consists of transmitted systems of symbols and patterns embodied with meaning. I believe this is our greatest strength; however, at times, it can be our Achilles heel.

EDUCATION: THE UN-KEPT PROMISE

Over the past four decades, education has become the un-kept promise of our society (Carlson and Gause, 2007). Children of color and in poverty continue to be the victims of failing schools and inadequately prepared teachers, and the recipients of inequitable learning conditions (Kozol, 1992). Given the present structure of the nations' public schools, the majority of ethnic/linguistic minorities will never realize their dreams—life, liberty, and the pursuit of happiness. Don't get me wrong—gains have been made and many minorities have benefited from programs and initiatives instituted by local, state, and federal legislation. However, as the population of the United States increases ethnically and racially, separation by class and race is more evident in our public schools, which will continue to leave children of color and children in poverty behind.

This book is a collection of thoughts, ideas, experiences, perspectives, theoretical frameworks, strategies, and resources for creating engaging, inviting and affirming learning communities for the 21st century. As a former public school teacher and administrator and a current professor in higher education working with PreK-20 leadership development, I believe it is important for education to be re-conceptualized as a "Birth to Elder" lifelong learning experience. This can only happen if a "seamless" educational experience is provided in this nation. I have witnessed the fragmentation of our educational institutions. Barriers exist between levels, grades, and content. Elementary, middle, high school, and college personnel do not interact or "see" how their work impacts and informs the other. The nature of the educational process disconnects students from the "essence of learning." When viewed from the macrolevel, each institution/school within the PreK-20 educational journey operates as its own mechanistic automaton. The curriculum is disconnected from real-life experiences and outcomes and, without this foundation, students are unable to become producers of their own knowledge.

Teaching is by far one of the most difficult professions. Educators are called upon to solve all of societal ills through the educational process. We are expected to teach students from very different and sometimes difficult backgrounds. Currently, teachers are expected to close not only the achievement gaps between demographic groups within the United States, but also the one that exists (on average) between U.S. students and students in some European and Asian countries. In many cities across America, there are far more students to teach and very little or adequate resources to teach them. Regardless of ethnicity, social class, race, or language, exceptional teachers provide opportunities for students to achieve and excel (Banks, 1996; Ladson-Billings, 1997; Gay, 2000). Given the budgetary cuts due to the recent global economic crisis, for the first time in many generations, educators are losing their jobs during one of the greatest teacher-shortages in the profession's history. Schools are closing across this nation at alarming rates. The lives of middle class America are disappearing right before our very eyes, and the number of children and families who are experiencing home foreclosures, unemployment, and increased poverty has grown exponentially (Gause, 2010). As dire as these conditions may be, we must utilize them to impact the future of our nation and world. This can only be done if we embrace diversity matters. Diversity matters require us to constantly seek opportunities to bridge differences by integrating our cultures, values, and beliefs with our daily practices. One of our practices as citizens of this democracy should be the act of critically reflecting on our individual as well as collective identities with the hope of promoting the common good for—all.

PERSONAL REFLECTION

In thinking about diversity work and writing this text, I must share my own personal reflection. I am a tenured faculty member of color who holds a doctoral and other advanced degrees from Tier 1 research institutions. Highly distinguished educational scholars from diverse ethnic and gendered identities mentored me. I have ample experience in leading, teaching, researching, and evaluating K-12 schools situated in a range of political, geographical, and cultural contexts. The additional elements of my identities are African American, male, same-affection-loving, Prophetic Christian, northerner, southerner, and Midwesterner. My praxis is rooted in collaborative activism, social justice, political struggle, and resistance. I did not come from a privileged background. I have two other siblings and, while growing up, my father worked in another state and my mother worked in various industries. She became ill and spent many of my elementary years in the hospital. I experienced poverty and under-employment in my home. My mother died when I was in the ninth grade. It took courage to get through those years. I was a fat kid who wore glasses and braces. One thing I do remember vividly is that I had caring teachers with multiple identities throughout my K-12 experience. They had courage for me when I did not have enough for myself.

Parker Palmer, in his work *The Courage to Teach: Exploring the Inner Landscape of a Teacher's Life*, explores this notion of courage. He asserts:

> The courage to teach is the courage to keep one's heart open in those very moments when the heart is asked to hold more than it is able so that teacher and students and subject can be woven into the fabric of community that learning, and living, require. (p. 11)

The terms "diversity," "equity," and "inclusion" are not just buzz words for my educational lexicon. I live those terms daily in multiple ways. I am a teacher, an African American male teacher and, above all else, this narrative is a part of who I am. This narrative is developed and re-developed through the process of education. The common good of our humanity lies within the learning process—learning of self and others. Education is that common good and serves as the foundation of our democracy.

I have been the only African American male faculty member in a university in the southeastern part of the United States who has struggled with recruiting and retaining faculty of color. As I journeyed toward promotion and tenure, I realized over time that there were very few faculty of color on my campus. I engaged in various questions and conversations regarding this with many of my colleagues from diverse backgrounds and, slowly, strides were made to make our campus more diverse as measured by ethnic and racial identifiers. Serving as one of the co-chairs on the Committee on Equity, Diversity, and Inclusion and continuing to do leadership work locally, nationally, and internationally in the area of inclusiveness, my experiences and the experiences of others brought about a realization: It is difficult to do diversity work and create inclusive communities systemically. Creating such communities is not just a matter of putting into place some cultural programming or creating more committees or student groups with visible physical difference, but eliminating policies, practices, and procedures that could be perceived as barriers or discriminatory.

Theorizing about creating inclusive communities is much different than actually putting theory into practice, and it can be painful in multiple ways for anyone who shares this vision or mission. It requires a collective effort by members who represent as many communities as possible within the learning community. It is the essence of collaborative activism. Conducting informal equity audits is a part of doing diversity and inclusive education (Skrla, Mckenzie, and Scheurich, 2009). Utilizing these audits is very engaging. I have conducted these audits in several educational communities for professional development, not only because of my research interests in the areas of equity, diversity, educational leadership, and gender studies, but also because many leaders of learning communities find these exercises valuable. I have learned to not give the perception that I am pushing my "own" agenda. Power is continually at work within institutions regardless of membership. Creating inclusive learning communities is inherent in how individuals approach diversity, social justice, racism, and their own biases. The majority of individuals I have encountered while conducting professional development sessions are usually operating out of a psychological view of racism. They believe if they could change what was in the heads of White people, particularly the top leadership of their institutions—who are all White and male, this would bring about a more inclusive and anti-oppressive environment. Educators often take this theoretical approach to dealing with racism. When utilizing this theoretical framework, resistance will always occur. I offer a structural analysis view of racism and diversity.

Racism is a structural construct or arrangement, if you will, among members of racial/ethnic groups. Racist institutions are controlled by the dominant culture, which develops, implements, and sustains practices, polices, and procedures that restrict the access of non-Whites to power and privilege. The evidence is clear in all institutions of the United States. We see this currently regarding health care, immigration reform, and access to higher education for children of undocumented workers. The debate within this country is growing exponentially.

DIVERSITY WORK IN HIGHER EDUCATION

Over the past two years, I have had the privilege of working with the Chancellor's Advisory Committee on Diversity, Equity, and Inclusion at a southeastern university. This group has conducted focus interviews of the following communities on their

5

campus: students with disabilities, the housekeeping staff, adult students, new faculty members, Gay, Lesbian, Bisexual, Transgender, Intersecting, Queer, Questioning, and Ally Students (GLBTIQQA), staff members, minority faculty members, minority students, international degree-seeking students, male students, and African American male students. (The work of this committee is presented in Chapter 4).

This has not come without many challenges. During my time with this group, I have witnessed workplace bullying and decisions that were made that were not equitable, and have had conversations with individuals who have been personally attacked via email by their colleagues and students both White and Black. Stanley (2006) provides an analysis of the literature on faculty of color at PWIs, noting that the paucity (there is a little) of empirical research mirrors the low numbers of this population at such institutions. In comparatively analyzing qualitative studies of faculty of color at PWIs, Stanley concludes that they are almost universally excluded, expected to only speak about diversity issues, expected to be a minority figurehead but not to engage in service directed at assisting minorities in some way, and expected, as scholars, to divorce their colored identity from their professional identity. The effects of affirmative action programs on hiring practices at PWIs in research is minimal; however, the literature does emphasize the fact that faculty of color, once hired, experience "cultural taxation"—additional work expectations that do not boost their chances of earning tenure and/or promotion. Roseboro & Gause (2009) argue that faculty of color face the unenviable burden of being perceived as "tokens" (e.g., unqualified for the job), being typecast (expected to only work at certain jobs), and of conducting illegitimate research when studying issues related to diversity (the "Brown on Brown" dilemma). Some faculty on this committee have discussed that they are serving in departments that claim to be about "social justice." One in particular has discussed the mere facilitation of his move to another department created the "appearance of insensitivities" by some in leadership roles within his college. He believe the lack of courtesy and privilege of being a tenured associate professor who has worked tirelessly on behalf of diversity, equity, and inclusion has gone unnoticed and is a form of retaliation. Is it racism? Is it a lack of cultural sensitivity? Is it White privilege? Is it the continued marginalization and disenfranchisement of the "other?" I call these experiences contractual benevolence. You are welcome to come to dinner at my house and sit at my table; but you better behave while at the table. There could be numerous reasons for many of my experiences and the experiences of others who are not members of the dominant culture; however, the root of it all goes back to power and hegemony.

What is so profound is that students and adults in both secondary and post-secondary learning communities across our nation and globe are having these same experiences. Wake County in North Carolina was celebrated for its public school diversity policy voted in a new school board with members running on a platform of dismantling the policy and enacting a neighborhood-based school attendance zone policy. Members from the community, NAACP, and media crammed in several school board hearings to protest this action, but to no avail; the new policy will have passed at the time of this book's publication. For these reasons, I provide you this text. All of this has been done in the name of stemming the cost of immigration or, better yet, to keep the "Mexicans" and "Blacks" from attending schools in neighborhoods where the home values are $575,000 to $1 million. This is not just occurring in North Carolina. The state of Arizona has passed legislation that allows law enforcement officers to stop anyone and request proof of U.S. citizenship. The governor of Arizona, Janet Napolitano, states this was done to prevent the increasing number of "illegal immigrants" from crossing the U.S.-Mexican border. All of this has been done in the name of "border control" and National Security. Governor Napolitano states that President Barack Obama and his administration are not doing their jobs when it comes to border security.

The political disturbances and re-articulation of what it means to be a member of the White establishment in today's America is evidenced by the multiple media outlets, "talking heads," and "political pundits" who utilize the airwaves to garner support for the days of old—no Black president, no illegal immigrants, no taxes on the wealthiest Americans, no racially balanced and/or mixed public schools, no Muslims or mosques at "ground zero," and, above all, no one getting ahead of the wealthy White power elite. As I re-think American democracy and the role of education in shaping this nation, diversity, equity, and inclusion/exclusion are all central to our history. Democracy is an enacted daily practice through which people interact and relate through personal, social, and professional routines with a primary focus on continuing the betterment of our humanity. Democracy does not seek to embrace hegemonic practices that maintain the status quo. It does not silence individuals and, at its core foundation, is the representation of difference in society. Putnam (1991) as cited in Gause (2008) stated "democracy is not just a form of social life among other workable forms of social life; it is the precondition for the full application of intelligence to the solution of social problems" (p. 145). It is valued collaboration from all walks of life that will improve a democracy truly based on unity. We must as a society and member of this global community move away from the dichotomies that exist when we think of diversity, equity, and inclusiveness. Through this work, I seek to focus not on Black or White, gay or straight, male or female paradigms; it is within the continuum of class, ethnicities, sexual identities, languages, gender, and the complexities of the intersections of the negotiations of our identities we as a country will gain our strength. The interconnectedness of our humanity depends on the understanding of our oneness. We all have the same color brain matter. The difference is not within our differences, but in how we connect our differences to forces of good or to forces of evil.

This book is written for everyone. This primer in its intent serves as a guide for those new and experienced with regard to diversity, equity, and inclusive education. It is not designed to be exhaustive, but to provide snapshots and synopses of people, events, and movements that have informed and/or impacted education locally and globally. This text also will provide educators seeking to transform learning communities into centers of inquiry and affirmation regardless of ability, ideology, and/or positionality tools, techniques, strategies, and resources. It is my hope this work is utilized in all arenas public and private, by undergraduate and graduate students, PreK-12 teachers and school administrators, educational leaders and policy makers, as well as higher education professionals and the business community.

The following chapters cover a plethora of paradigms, constructs, and ideologies. The affirmation of difference from my vantage point requires a more intricate look into the relationships between class, privilege, sexual identity, race/ethnicity, positionality, gender, ability, spirituality/faith/religion, culture, and, above all, power and education. It is my intent to open the discourses surrounding multiculturalism and pluralism, particularly as they relate to developing engaging, affirming, and transformational professional learning communities that move beyond tokenism and hegemony. In Chapter 2, while journeying through the evolution of multiculturalism and multi-cultural education, I (re)position the constructs of diversity, equity, and inclusion against the backdrop of critical pedagogy, critical theory, and cultural studies. I also present those individuals, movements, and events that were significant to creating an activist nation with global impact. Throughout American history, individuals who sought equality and equity committed acts of resistance. These acts led to new Federal and state legislation, judicial cases, and laws that would forever change our nation. Scholars and educators in the 1970s began to utilize the terms multiculturalism and multicultural education. Artists and writers began utilizing the terms in the 1980s. In the 1990s, multiculturalism and multicultural education evolved into diversity, equity, and inclusion and were the foundational forces for transforming popular culture.

Chapter 3 explores how technology, particularly the evolution of the Internet, Smartphone technology, and social networking, has informed the way individuals make sense of their lived experiences. I present a case study to capture many of these elements. Chapter 4 presents perspectives regarding collaborative activism. I discuss the efforts of higher education institutions to become more inclusive and the struggles public schools within urban and rural environments are encountering with their change in demographics.

Chapter 5 is a journey into the thoughts and perspectives of educators of color with regard to diversity, equity, and inclusive education. Chronicling the personal and professional lives of educators through their narratives provides a scope for understanding the difficulties in achieving integration. By providing parts of my own narrative, I offer pedagogy of hope.

Most importantly, I conclude with a plethora of resources for further discovery and inspiration. This section includes websites, references, journals, timelines, legal information, and a bibliography for the reader to continue to engage, question, and critique policies and best practices for creating and sustaining professional learning communities that are engaging, affirming, and transformative.

GLOSSARY

Collaborative activism: Different groups collectively working together systemically without regard to difference, values, and beliefs to transform their communities. These individuals view this work as counter-hegemonic and anti-oppressive. They seek to eliminate barriers and biases.

Contractual benevolence: Members of the White dominant culture extending an invitation to a person of color to participate in various settings to include employment, however, with limitations. They must adhere to all "codes" and not question or critique inequities. For example, they are invited to dinner, but they must behave at the dinner table; however, they have no idea what is inappropriate behavior.

Critical pedagogy: Teaching approach or practice that encourages students to deconstruct, critique, and question taken-for-granted assumptions, values, norms, and beliefs. The focus is on questioning power and domination in institutional practices. Relationships exist between teaching and learning, which requires a continuous process of unlearning, learning, and relearning.

Critical theory: A social theory developed out of the Frankfurt School that focuses on the critique and examination of society and culture. It moves beyond the role of traditional theory—understanding and explaining to derive solutions to change society.

Cultural sensitivity: Being aware that cultural similarities and differences exist and impact behavior, learning, and values.

Cultural studies: The academic field or discipline grounded in critical theory. It is concerned with the messages and medium of popular culture and how they relate to constructs of social class, ethnicity, nationality, ideology, gender, and sexuality.

Culture: a) socially constructed and lived experiences translated from the meaning making of individuals; that is, how individuals view themselves daily as participants in the world around them and how they make sense of those daily interactions; b) transmitted systems of symbols and patterns embodied with meaning.

Democracy: An enacted daily practice through which people interact and relate through personal, social, and professional routines with a primary focus on continuing the betterment of our humanity.

Digital migration: The interfacing and transfer of information digitally across multiple mediums to include servers, satellites, cable, and fiber optics.

Disenfranchisement: Revoking the right to vote of an individual or group of individuals or rendering that vote ineffective or less effective. Disenfranchisement may occur implicitly through intimidation or explicitly by institutional systems or structures to include laws and policies.

Diversity: Representations of real or perceived identity constructs based on religion, ideology, political belief, sex, creed, color, national origin, age, socioeconomic status, gender identity/expression, physical characteristics, sexual orientation/identity, able-ness, parental status, (dis)ability, weight, cultural capital, height, and/or race.

Equity: Distribution of resources based upon what the individual and/or the collective needs without regard to demographics or differences.

Equity audit: Systematic approach to assessing the degree of equity or inequity within institutions, organizations, and/or schools.

Globalization: Process by which regional societies, cultures, and economies have become integrated through a global network of communication, transportation, and commerce.

Hegemony: The cultural, political, ideological, and economic power exerted over a group or groups of individuals by a dominant group regardless of consent.

Inclusion: A 1990s educational movement whereby students with special education needs spent time with non-disabled students. Students with special needs were "mainstreamed" into "regular" classrooms and other educational settings.

Inclusive education: A radical democratic social-justice-oriented approach to creating, developing, and sustaining inquiry-based, bias-free learning communities; the development of engaging, affirming, and dynamic learning communities that empower all members regardless of identity difference to achieve and excel by eliminating all barriers to include policies and practices.

Integration: The process of levelling barriers by ending systematic segregation and creating equal and equitable opportunities regardless of race, social class, sexuality, disability, value, morals, beliefs, religion, or ideology. A social construct that draws on diverse traditions and cultures, rather than bringing a minority into the majority.

Internationalization: A process of increasing movement of commerce into global markets; the outcome of economic, social, cultural, and educational globalization.

Marginalization: Placed into a position that is neither outside of the dominant culture nor accepted by most people.

Other: Individuals who have been excluded or subordinated by society because they are perceived to not fit the cultural values or norms of that society; a result of the processes of exclusion by the dominant culture.

Positionality: The way in which one is situated within the intersections of their identities and the power and politics of race/ethnicity, language, class, culture, gender, sexuality, ability, and other socio-cultural-political-environmental forces.

Power: The measurement of an entity's ability to control self and others.

Same-affection-loving: Spiritual attraction for individuals without considering their biological sex or gender. The affection of soul connection speaks to the desire for another human being without body consideration; physical appearance, cognitive abilities, and social/cultural capital are not considered during initial meeting.

Social justice: A philosophy and movement that investigates, critiques, and poses solutions for issues that reproduce and generate social inequities.

Tokenism: Policies, behaviors, and practices of limited inclusion of members who are not the majority, creating a false appearance of inclusive practices and a diversity community. Examples: Purposely including a Black character in an all-White cast, including women in a traditional male environment, allowing space for limited use of a language other than English, purposely including one person from another ethnic background or ability group within the majority context.

White establishment: The understood status quo of being a White, Protestant, male heterosexual with the power-base to rule, dominate, and control all economic, social, political, and cultural resources.

White privilege: A conceptualization of racial inequities based on critical race theory that speak to the advantages White people accrue from society based on their "Whiteness" juxtaposed with the disadvantages that people of color experience.

MOVEMENTS, PEOPLE, AND EVENTS

Creating a New World

What the elites of today want is for the people not to think.

Paulo Freire

While the new millennium arrived with great economic prosperity, citizens of the United States currently face a weaker economy, a depressed housing market, costly wars in Iraq and Afghanistan, and all the old problems of the late 20th century—power, race, identity, violence, and ethical breaches. Current challenges for educators include: 1) accountability; 2) high-stakes testing; 3) increases in immigrant population; 4) youth violence; 5) inadequate funding; 6) the search for meaning; and 7) the re-segregation of public schools along class/racial lines. I believe these challenges have broad implications for public schooling, and I utilize them to platform my inquiry into democratic education and social justice.

The American public educational system has fostered and continues to foster the inadequate preparation of students of color and those in poverty. This inadequate preparation is often fostered in highly impacted schools with high poverty and high need. The teachers and school administrators are often in need of additional resources. Many of the schools are in the same district and often no more than two miles from schools with affluence and privilege. High-need schools across America are watching their resources go into schools which often do not need the additional support. Teacher education programs and learning communities in general often focus on privileged perceptions of the dominant culture. This is evident in many of the curriculum programs that stress "tech-prep," "groupings," and "tracking." Having spent the past 30 years in public schools in various parts of the United States in varying positions, it is my personal perception that a privileged White middle-class work force continues to enter multiethnic public schools with their own worldview of educating the masses with little regard for the masses' own worldview.

I have worked in settings where the perception was White teachers are "all-knowing," African American teachers have "limited knowledge," and Black kids are "under-achievers, but the gifted ones are exceptions." Many educators across this country are calling for more culturally responsive teaching as a means of providing a quality education for the children of this nation. There are some scholars and policy-makers who believe, by engaging this practice, educators will begin to critique the fundamental issues of power, better understand the "lived" experiences of their students and how the relationship between these experiences and the greater societal forces impact learning which ultimately affects schools. According to Gay (2000)

Teachers practice culturally responsive teaching when an equity pedagogy is implemented. They use instructional materials and practices that incorporate important aspects of the family and community culture of their students. Culturally responsive teachers also use the "cultural knowledge, prior experiences, frames of reference, and performance styles of ethnically diverse students to make learning encounters more relevant to and effective for them." (p. 29)

Culturally responsive teaching asks how and why knowledge gets constructed the way that it does and how affirming the cultures of students increases their learning potential. Not doing so legitimizes enculturation, which marginalizes those students who are not members of the dominant culture. We see this to be very evident in educating "people of color" and/or "others" who are not a part of the privileged class. For example, when educating Black children, often the culture of this group as a potential force for political, economic, and social development is given very little attention during the "schooling" process. Many times, students are perceived to be passive recipients of knowledge transmitted from the teacher. In this construct, teachers make deposits of information that the students are to receive and store for later retrieval and the more students work at storing these deposits and not reflect critically upon them or develop "critical consciousness," the more they are not able to intervene in the world as transformers of that world.

Entering the last year of the first decade of the 21st century provided a moment of hope and optimism. Reflecting back now on *Time* Magazine's declaration of the 2000s as the worst decade ever recorded in history may now be oxymoronic. Yes, the 2000s were filled with Ponzi schemes, economic meltdowns, natural disasters of catastrophic proportions, the attack on the World Trade Center, and the power of the United States Government to utilize fear to pass the Patriot Act and utilize this landmark legislation to violate the rights of everyday citizens. Under the guise of terrorism, Americans born and/or naturalized were policed at alarming rates.

Those who appeared to be Latino based upon racial profiling found themselves and their citizenship being called into question. Local, state, and national law enforcement utilized these opportunities to create a culture of fear while politicians debated our nation's policies regarding immigration. What I found most troubling is that the United States of America is a land of immigrants. According to the 2006 U. S. Census Bureau, approximately 1% of the U.S. population identified as Native American while 98% of the U.S. population identified as White, African American, Hispanic, and Asian American. What is striking is that, in the early 1600s, the Native American population range was 10–90 million before the Europeans arrived on the American continent. A critique of U.S. history reveals that, at present, 98% of the U.S. population is made up of descendants of immigrants. Multiculturalism is the affirmation of multiple ethnic cultures, religious beliefs, and group identities without specifically promoting the values of one group over the other. It is in direct contrast to social integration, where people often give up their own identities and assimilate into another culture.

Multicultural education gained popularity in the field of education in the late 1970s and early 1980s, offering a different point of view on educational practices and policies with regard to acculturation. The population of the United States was growing rapidly and a noted shift in population demographics occurred, due largely to the increase in the number of immigrants after the passage of the Immigration Act of 1965 and successive immigration laws. This legislation reopened the doors to the United States to immigrants again for the first time since the Immigration Act of 1924 closed them. The percentage of immigrants arriving to the U.S. in 1924 had been cut close to zero. The percentage of foreign-born residents in 1910 was 15% and had dropped steadily to 4.7% in 1970.

In 2007, the total population of the United States was 301.6 million, which included 38.1 million foreign born, representing 12.6% of the total population. Approximately 15% of the total population reported a Hispanic origin. The term "melting pot" was utilized to describe the United States as a place comprised of individuals who immigrated here and adopted all things American. This included learning American English and forgetting one's native language, accepting and espousing American values and belief systems, and taking on American cultures and rituals to include "baseball, hotdog, apple pie, and Chevrolet." Immigrants were encouraged to engage in this process of assimilation to gain access to the rights, resources, and privileges that come with being an American. Those who engaged in this acculturation forgot their native language or languages, disengaged from their own religious customs and practices, and disavowed themselves from their native cultural rituals or beliefs. Presently, the term "salad bowl" is in vogue. This term espouses the idea that all individuals and groups retain their various cultural practices, rituals, beliefs, values, and customs. Doing so enhances the tenets of the founding of this nation—freedom and democracy. Each distinctive group in this nation along with their multiple identities and values shape America into one collective identity: *e pluribus unum*—out of many one. This Latin phrase is located on the Great Seal of the United States. The salad bowl metaphor reveals that each ingredient of a salad has its own unique flavor. By bringing together all of the ingredients in a salad, a new and different flavor is created. The greatest strength of our nation is found within our inclusivity.

WHAT LAND OF THE FREE, HOME OF THE BRAVE?

Providing synopses of history, people, and movements is ambitious at best but often difficult. Deciding what to highlight and how much is a gruelling task; what is not presented, highlighted, or documented is the usually the most intriguing. The availability of so much data and virtual texts through online databases is exciting. This chapter will journey through the evolution of multiculturalism and multicultural education; however, I problematize these constructs against the backdrop of critical pedagogy, critical theory, and cultural studies, which all have foundations within the Frankfurt School. Doing so will challenge educators and those who inform educational policy to create dynamic, engaging, and affirming learning communities where inquiry and knowledge production are central to the educative process. The following chapter provides a context for technology and diversity and the final chapter provides resources and data sources for your further investigation; because of this, I believe a review of the 20th century would be most important. The last

100 years of American history, particularly in the areas of diversity, equity, and inclusive education, are profound. As you engage this chapter, critically reflect on your own knowledge of events and "lived" experiences. Question your own thoughts, feelings, and memories of lessons learned about the information and allow multiple epiphanies to take place.

The original 13 colonies of the United States declared their independence from Great Britain when the Continental Congress adopted a statement of declaration on July 4, 1776. The second sentence of this document is often hailed as the most profound sweeping statement of individual human rights in the history of humankind:

> We hold these truths to be self-evident, that all men are created equal, that they are endowed by their creator with certain unalienable Rights, that among these are Life, Liberty, and the Pursuit of Happiness.

Marginalized individuals and groups have utilized this passage to protect their rights and freedoms. Abraham Lincoln often espoused the idea the Declaration of Independence is a statement of principles by which the United States Constitution should be interpreted. The United States Constitution is the supreme law of our nation and establishes a framework for governance and the relationship of the federal government to the citizens of this nation, the states, and all individuals located within our borders. The Constitution was adopted on September 17, 1787, by the Constitutional Convention and ratified in each U. S. state. The first ten amendments are known as the Bill of Rights. I have included both the Declaration of Independence and the United States Constitution in Chapter 6 for your review.

When both of these documents were developed and ratified, women and persons of diverse racial/ethnic backgrounds were not signatories or members of the ratifying bodies. Women did not have the right to vote and persons of color were considered property. White heterosexual men were the power block. Women's suffrage occurred many years after the passage of this document; however, women did have an impact on these times. The 19th Amendment to the United States Constitution giving women the right to vote was introduced in Congress in 1878; however, it was not ratified until 1920. The origins of the modern women's suffrage movement are attributed to 18th century France. Women's suffrage has been granted throughout global history many times; however, it was not until 1979, when the United Nations adopted the Convention on the Elimination of All Forms of Discrimination Against Women, that universal suffrage took effect. There are still countries within our global society where women do not have the right to vote, own property, handle their own affairs, and/or have a "voice" in the socio-cultural and political arenas of their land. Currently in America, there are laws protecting the rights of women; however, women still earn less then men and, in many parts of this country, women continue to have inadequate health care and limited legal protections when it comes to domestic violence. The issue here is patriarchy and how men and women are defined in this country.

DOLLS, JACKS, AND TONKA TRUCKS

Sexual identity, gender expression, and sexual orientation are all under suspicion in the United States, particularly if you are not a White male heterosexual. Based upon the socio-cultural dynamics of what is defined as male or female in our society, gender has little to do with an individual's actual biological sex or sexual identity/ orientation. Sex is chromosomal, while gender incorporates socio-cultural, political, and behavioral performances that are ever evolving. While sex is biological and can be determined by a simple test, gender has more to do with identity and common notions of femininity and masculinity. Gender does not always correspond to biological sex. Gender is fluid and not a static concept. Our human behaviors and their interpretation by those who witness them speak to how gender is constructed, enacted, performed, and contextualized. To be male or female means a pattern of behaviors must be engaged and read for the production of gender. There are men who like to express themselves as women and there are women who like to express themselves as men. This nation continues to be skeptical and abrasive towards nonconforming gender identities. Currently same-sex marriage is only recognized by five of the 50 states, one Federal district and one Native American tribe or nation. They are as follows: Connecticut, Iowa, Massachusetts, New Hampshire, Vermont, Washington, D.C., and the Coquille Indian Tribe in Oregon. Interestingly enough, our democracy and nation is only 234 years old, and many of the following countries have existed much longer legally recognize same-sex marriage: Argentina, Belgium, Canada, Iceland, Netherlands, Norway, Portugal, South African, Spain, and Sweden. Many people believe to allow same-sex marriage would be an assault on masculinity.

Men in this country historically are continually defined by the following masculinities: physical masculinity, functional masculinity, sexual masculinity, emotional masculinity, intellectual masculinity, and interpersonal masculinity. These definitions and constructs continue to impact the United States in the area of domestic policy, governance, and foreign diplomacy.

DISCOURSES ON MULTICULTURALISM AND DIVERSITY

Public discourse in the United States on multiculturalism and diversity in education has reached an all-time backlash. Growing discontent on the implementation of diversity policies is televised across television networks and the World Wide Web. In 2010, Texas adopted new textbooks that eliminated "key" historical information regarding the role of persons of color in this nation. Wake County Schools of Raleigh, North Carolina eliminated their diversity policy, which included bussing students away from their neighborhood schools to reach racial and social class "balance" in many of their schools; and several states across this nation closed schools that were overwhelming minority and high-poverty to save their budgets.

Clearly, conversations regarding diversity, equity, and inclusion, particularly in educational arenas, have been reduced to the bottom line: "what can we do to save our budget and eliminate costs?" Interestingly enough, educators in the late 20th century focused on the "how can we all get along?" and forgot to have conversations regarding the economic, social, political, and cultural forces we as human beings bring to the "table of equality." I opened this book with an introduction that included some of my personal perspectives with regard to my own lived experiences not only as an educator, but a social justice educator/activist. Diversity and multiculturalism have evolved into politically correct terms utilized by people to not appear racist, sexist, or homophobic. Yes, state and Federal legislation have been enacted to protect the rights of those who are not members of the White dominant culture; however, people of color in the United States continue to not receive equal wages for equal work. They continue to have higher rates of poverty, more inadequate health care, and higher rate of school non-completion than their White counterparts.

Early multiculturalists, political actors, and educators who were involved in the early diversity movement did not call for an examination of White privilege or cultural hegemony. Their main concern was how to get this nation of immigrants to come together and "friend" one another. The development of this nation is filled with the blood, sweat, and tears of the Native Americans who "friended" the newcomers to eventually be forced off of their land and put on reservations. The colonizers brought people of color in chains—taken from their homelands to work the land—while they themselves became robber barons. As we cast our eyes across the 2010 horizon, we can see not much has changed. Everyone has some perspective regarding diversity—herein lies the problem. Diversity, multiculturalism, and multicultural education are empty of their own theoretical underpinnings. There is not one conceptual/theoretical framework, taxonomy/paradigm, or school curriculum/philosophy that serves as the foundation for creating citizens who affirm difference.

The premise of this book is found in critical diversity and multiculturalism. Much of this work evolves from critical theory, critical pedagogy, and cultural studies. Critical theory is a broad tradition based upon the use of the critique as a method of investigation. The primary characteristic of this school of thought, which has its roots in the Frankfurt School, is that social theory, regardless of whether it is reflected towards educational research, philosophy, literature, art, or business, should play a vital role in changing the world and not be heavily concerned with just recording information. The Frankfurt School of "critical theory" was regarded by orthodox Marxists as "revisionist" partly because it criticized economics and crude materialism and partly because of its eclecticism. The most notable theorists connected with the Frankfurt School were Theodor Adorno, Herbert Marcuse, and Max Horkheimer—all committed Marxists—who were associated with the Institute for Social Research, which was founded in Frankfurt in 1923 but shifted in 1933 to New York.

Cultural studies is a transdisciplinary approach to "making sense" of the world. Cultural studies is not bound to or based on disciplines. It is focused on issues regarding the intersections of race/ethnicity, class, gender, sexuality, national identity, colonialism, cultural critical pedagogy, cultural popularism, and textuality. Cultural studies' foundation is formulated by the political and the ideological. It rejects traditional notions of teaching as technique or sets of skills. Teaching is a cultural practice only to be understood through considerations of history, politics, power, and culture. Cultural studies is not concerned with issues surrounding certification, assessment, and accountability. The emphasis is how knowledge, texts, and cultural products are developed, mass-produced, mediated, and consumed.

EVOLUTION OF MULTICULTURAL EDUCATION AND DIVERSITY

Educators and the very institution of education operate from and are constructed from social and historical relations of power. Because of this, privileged narrative spaces are constructed for some social groups (dominant culture) and a space for inequality and subordination are constructed for the "other;" this was understood by Carter G. Woodson and Jesse E. Moorland. These scholars established the Association for the Study of Negro Life and History. W. E. B. DuBois and Charles C. Wesley also were scholars and pioneers of ethnic studies through their research and books on the history and culture of African Americans. Dr. Carter G. Woodson founded the *Journal of Negro History* and the *Negro History Bulletin* as means to share his research and provide curriculum materials to be integrated into the curricula of segregated schools. He also provided these venues as a means for African American scholars and teachers at historically Black colleges and universities to empower their students with the knowledge of their own history.

During the 1920s, some scholars were writing and training teachers in intercultural education. This movement had an international emphasis. Many textbooks were rewritten to provide an international perspective. Many teachers called for their curriculum to be more relevant to the modern world. Post World War I, the Harlem Renaissance, and the age of industrialization contributed greatly to the intercultural movement. As the United States began to expand its global footprint and become a land of immigrants, the goal of the intercultural movement was to make the dominant population tolerant and accepting of individuals who did not look like them nor share their same cultural rituals. Proponents of the intercultural movement believed educating the citizens of the United States to be more accepting of first- and second-generation immigrants would maintain national unity and social control. As the intercultural movement grew, interculturalists supported the appreciation of difference, but failed to affirm and promote multiple collective identities.

As the United States entered and exited World War II and following the Holocaust, tensions grew and remained high and various organizations were developed to improve intergroup relations. The creation of Jewish organizations, e.g., the Anti-Defamation League and the American Jewish Committee, provided forms of leadership to ease tensions and collaborate with non-Jews. The goal was to reduce the anti-Semitic sentiment that existed during that time. Progressive educational leaders such as Hilda Taba and Lloyd A. Cook promoted inter- and intra-group relations to develop tolerance for new immigrants, African Americans, and members of other racial/ethnic groups.

The 1960s ushered in desegregation due to the 1954 landmark decision of the United States Supreme Court in *Brown v. Board of Education of Topeka*. The decision by the Court declared state laws establishing separate public schools for Black and White students and denying Black students equal educational opportunities were unconstitutional. Also during this time, cultural, racial, and ethnic differences were being described as deficits. Students of color and White impoverished students were considered to be lacking the academic aptitude to succeed. Politicians, policymakers, scholars and some educators believed these students did not possess enough cultural capital to keep up with their White counterparts. The Moynihan Report contributed to this misnomer and programs like Head Start, compensatory education, and special education programs were developed in order to make up for these deficits. President Lyndon Baines Johnson on June 4, 1965 delivered the commencement address at Howard University in Washington, D.C. Howard, considered one of the most prestigious of the historically black colleges and universities, was the perfect location to utilize data from the Moynihan report to encourage the Black community to do more with regard to the Black family, so President Johnson thought. It became a point of contention and forever changed how African Americans viewed the government. A copy of his speech is presented in chapter 6.

Compensatory and special education programs of today found their beginnings in the Elementary and Secondary Educational Act (ESEA). This statute was enacted by Congress April 11, 1965 as sweeping legislation to fund education within the United States. It is often regarded as the first step to nationalizing public schools in America; however, public schools are the responsibility of each individual state as noted by the Tenth Amendment of the United States Constitution.

The United States entered a tumultuous time period during the 1960s. During this time, President John F. Kennedy, his brother Attorney General Robert F. Kennedy, and the "Drum Major for Justice," civil rights leader Dr. Martin Luther King, were assassinated. The United States had entered war with Vietnam, the struggle for civil rights and gay rights both reached a crescendo with the assassination of Dr. Martin Luther King and the Stonewall Riots in New York City. With regard to all of the protest and demands for equal rights, participants only demanded what they believed was granted under the United States Constitution. I have included a copy of the Constitution and all amendments in Chapter 6 of this text as a resource for your review.

The riots of the 1960s emerged into self-awareness and "free love" which ushered in the Age of Aquarius in the 1970s. This time period saw a renewed interest in ethnic and cultural studies, intergroup relations, and calls for ending all discriminatory practices. Title IX was passed in 1972, granting equal access to educational programs receiving financial assistance in higher education. Public educational institutions could no longer discriminate on the basis of race or gender. This legislation covered course offerings, scholarships, financial aid, athletics, recruitment, admissions, and any other activity.

Shirley Chisholm, the first Black woman elected to Congress, in 1964, became the major-party candidate for president of the United States. She received 152 first-ballot votes at the 1972 Democratic National Convention. In 1973, the United States Supreme Court issued its decision in *Roe v. Wade*, which upheld a woman's constitutional right to privacy extended to her decision to have a safe and legal abortion in the first trimester of pregnancy. It also upheld this decision had to be balanced with the state's position of protecting prenatal life and the health of the mother. This is one of the most significant decisions historically by the United States Supreme Court and remains one of the most controversial 37 years later.

The 1980s were indeed a time of great censorship, fear, and political conservativism. After the presidency of Jimmy Carter and the Iran-Hostage situation, Ronald Wilson Reagan, an actor and former governor of California, became the 40th President of the United States. AIDS became front and center in global health and would forever change how domestic health policy is debated in this country. During the 1980s, growing disparities between the wealthy and those in poverty grew immensely. A surge in the underground economy, including drug trafficking, grew exponentially.

Inner-city neighborhoods were filled with violence, death, and destruction. Draconian drug laws were passed to end the flow of illegal drugs into the United States; however, the outcome of these laws was that a disproportionate number of Black and Latino men were placed into the penal system. This decade also ushered in the information age. Computers and their use were became more common in educational arenas and commerce.

The 1990s saw the continuation of Reaganomics as George H.W. Bush became the 41st President of the United States. President Bush, during his term, signed legislation giving the government power to collect data on hate crimes. He also declared war on Iraq and the Persian Gulf. A Democrat was elected to the nation's highest office by the mid-decade. President Clinton was considered the "first Black President," although he was White and wealthy. On March 31, 1994, President Clinton signed into law The Goals 2000: Educate America Act. This law provided resources to states to and communities to ensure that all students reach their full potential and was based on principles of outcome-based education. The goals were as follows:

– By the year 2000…

– All children in America will start school ready to learn.

– The high school graduation rate will increase to at least 90%.

– All students will leave grades 4, 8, and 12 having demonstrated competency over challenging subject matter including English, mathematics, science, foreign languages, civics and government, economics, the arts, history, and geography, and every school in America will ensure that all students learn to use their minds well, so they may be prepared for responsible citizenship, further learning, and productive employment in our nation's modern economy.

– United States students will be first in the world in mathematics and science achievement.

– Every adult American will be literate and will possess the knowledge and skills necessary to compete in a global economy and exercise the rights and responsibilities of citizenship.

– Every school in the United States will be free of drugs, violence, and the unauthorized presence of firearms and alcohol and will offer a disciplined environment conducive to learning.

– The nation's teaching force will have access to programs for their continued improvement of their professional skills and the opportunity to acquire the knowledge and skills needed to instruct and prepare all American students for the next century.

– Every school will promote partnerships that will increase parental involvement and participation in promoting the social, emotional, and academic growth of children.

http://www.ncrel.org/sdrs/areas/issues/envrnmnt/stw/sw0goals.htm

Goals 2000 is considered the precursor to No Child Left Behind, which was signed into law by President George W. Bush on January 8, 2002.

No Child Left Behind (NCLB) is considered to be the reincarnation of the Elementary and Secondary Education Act of 1965, which created the Title I Federal aid program aimed at reducing achievement gaps between rich and poor and among the races. NCLB ties Federal dollars to draconian penalties for any school that cannot meet a series of one-size-fits-all standards. These penalties hurt schools that often are the greatest challenges—high need and high poverty. The penalties are based upon a reporting system entitled Adequate Yearly Progress (AYP). Under NCLB, all students in grades 3–8 and in one grade in high school must be tested once a year in reading and mathematics. Students are expected to score at the "proficient" level or above on state-administered tests by 2014.

Subgroups of students, including low-income, Black, Hispanic, special needs students and English language learners, also must meet AYP standards. If they do not, the entire school has failed. In addition to test-score requirements, schools and subgroups must meet attendance or competency determination requirements. Under these rules, 95% of students must take the test; average daily attendance in a K-8 school must be 92%, and 70% of high school students must pass test requirements for graduation. A school that fails to make AYP for two consecutive years is labelled "in need of improvement." Those that receive Federal Title I funds—funds allocated to schools that serve a requisite number of low-income students—face sanctions that increase over time. After two years, sanctioned schools must give parents the choice of sending their children to another school in the district, with transportation costs paid out of Title I dollars. After five years, a school faces "corrective action." After seven years, a school must be "restructured" with options including state take-over, conversion to a charter school, management by a private company, or other unspecified "major restructuring." A Title I school faces sanctions whether the failure to meet AYP is based on aggregate scores or scores from one of the seven subgroups.

Scholar and multiculturalist Dr. James A. Banks published in 1995 *Multicultural Education: Historical Development, Dimensions, and Practice*. In this work, he presented the Five Dimensions of Multicultural Education. These dimensions have been utilized by school districts across the U.S. to develop projects, programs, and courses in multicultural education. The five dimensions are: 1) content integration, 2) knowledge construction process, 3) prejudice reduction, 4) equity pedagogy, and 5) an empowering school culture/social structure. Each dimension is conceptually distinct; in practice, they are interrelated and overlap. Understanding diversity and multiculturalism present multiple unique and different manifestations based upon the contexts in which they are operationalized. Scholars and critical pedagogues Shirley Steinberg and Joseph Kincheloe moved the discourse further along the continuum and analyzed the evolution of multicultural education through the lens of critical pedagogy and offered five frames regarding diversity in public discourse. They realized, until there exist a critique of Whiteness as ethnicity and the development of a unifying critical taxonomy of diversity, we will never move beyond the superficial. In Steinberg (2009), Kincheloe, Steinberg et al. (1998), and Kincheloe

and Steinberg (1997), five frames were found in public discourse regarding multi-cultural education:
- Conservative diversity practice and multiculturalism or monoculturalism
- Liberal diversity practice and multiculturalism
- Pluralist diversity practice and multiculturalism
- Left-essentialist diversity practice and multiculturalism
- Critical diversity and multiculturalism.

The close of the 20th century brought many triumphs and tragedies. On September 11, 2001, the nation was struck to its core by terrorists with attacks on the Pentagon in Virginia and the World Trade Center in New York and the great courage of passengers who took over a plane held by terrorists and brought it down in Pennsylvania. Many issues regarding religious freedom in the United States and abroad were called into question. This attack has often been attributed to Jihad. The ending of the first decade of the millennium and the election of the nation's first self-identified African American President Barack Hussein Obama, who has a multi-racial genealogy, continue to conjure up issues regarding race, social, class, and identity in America and the world. If we ever need a time for critical consciousness—the time is now.

GLOSSARY

Acculturation: The exchange of cultural paradigms from the first-hand continuous contact of different cultural groups resulting in the original patterns of either or both groups being altered, while the groups remain distinct.

Age of Aquarius: This term in popular culture refers to the hippie and New Age movements of the 1970s. This period was filled with drug experimentation, rock music, and sexual revolution.

ADA: The Americans with Disabilities Act was passed by Congress and signed into law on July 26, 1990. A civil rights law that prohibits, under certain conditions, discrimination based on disability.

AIDS: Acquired Immune Deficiency Syndrome, a disease of the human immune system that has no cure. It is contracted via direct contact with infected mucous membranes, blood, or semen. There are 33.2 million people living with the disease worldwide. It is considered a pandemic and 2.1 million people, including 330,000 children, have died from the disease. AIDS and its cause, HIV, were first recognized in the United States in 1981 by the Centers for Disease Control in the early 1980s.

Ally: Individuals who work to reduce homophobia and/or transphobia in their communities by educating themselves and others; they support individuals with gender identities in political, social, and cultural arenas.

Bisexual: A person who is attracted to people regardless of gender.

Civil rights: The rights of personal liberty guaranteed by the 13th and 14th Amendments to the U. S. Constitution and by acts of Congress. A movement calling for the desegregation of schools, bussing companies, restaurants, hotels, and other public venues by African Americans. This movement involved marches, sit-ins, protests, and other forms of resistance.

Colonizers: Individuals who migrate, settle, and occupy land bringing their own customs, rituals, beliefs, values, morals, and ideologies and forcing those who are present to accept them. Historically, these individuals have taken possession of the land by force.

Compensatory education: Provision of special services to students who have limited educational or economic opportunities with the goal of reducing the educational gap between them and their advantaged peers.

Content integration: A technique in which teachers use examples and content from a variety of cultures and groups to illustrate key concepts, principles, generalizations, and theories in their subject area or discipline.

Cultural capital: The possession and or access to endowments or resources that provide an advantage to individuals, groups, and families to succeed in American culture. Wealth, language competence, academic competence, and the ability to navigate institutional structures and systems are considered elements of cultural capital.

Culturally responsive teaching: A pedagogy that views and affirms the cultures, values, and experiences of students as strengths and reflects the students' "lived" experiences in the teaching process.

Diverse: Exhibiting characteristics that set individuals apart from one another.

Emotional masculinity: Unemotional, stoic, and/or refusing to cry.

Empowering school culture/social structure: Restructuring the culture and organization of the school so students from diverse racial, ethnic, socioeconomic, and language groups experience equality.

Equity pedagogy: A technique in which teachers modify their teaching in ways that will facilitate the academic achievement of students from diverse racial, cultural, socioeconomic, and language groups. This includes using a variety of teaching styles and approaches that are consistent with the range of learning styles within various cultural and ethnic groups.

ESEA: The Elementary and Secondary Education Act is Federal legislation that provides resources and funds primary and secondary education in the U.S. It is the first broad, sweeping statute regarding education in U.S. history. It has been re-authorized every five years since its inception with new and/or additional changes and is currently known as NCLB, No Child Left Behind.

Enculturation: Acquiring the characteristics of a given culture, becoming competent in its rituals, customs, language, "ways of being," learning, and behaving. This process usually begins at birth and is often done for assimilation purposes.

Equality: A state of being in which one cultural group is not inferior or superior to another and all groups have access to the same benefits of society regardless of group membership.

Exclusion: The act or process of denying an individual membership or the opportunity to participate and or engage with the group.

Frankfurt School: A school of neo-Marxist interdisciplinary social theory, associated with the Institute of Social Research at the University of Frankfurt am Main. This school serves as the founding place of critical theory.

Functional masculinity: Being the breadwinner and provider for the family.

Gay: An individual who is attracted to individuals of the same sex.

Gay rights: A movement calling for full acceptance of individuals with non-conforming sexual identities/orientations, gender identities, and queer identities.

Gender: A set of complicated socio-cultural political practices whereby human bodies are transformed into "men" and "women." This term also deems what society believes to be "masculine" or "feminine."

GLBTIQQA: An acronym that stands for "Gay, Lesbian, Bisexual, Transgender, Intersex, Queer, Questioning, and Allied." The acronym is designed to be inclusive of alternative sexual identities and orientations; however, the categories in the 21st century are appearing to become more disrupted and dissolved by members of this diverse community.

Hispanic: A term to denote the people and culture of countries formerly ruled by the Spanish Empire; often utilized by the U.S. Census Bureau.

Immigrants: Those individuals who are introduced into a new setting, habitat, or population.

Immigration: The process of introducing an individual into a new population and/or setting.

Inclusivity: A system of measures designed to quantify and/or qualify the acts and processes of affirming identity difference of individuals and groups by eliminating barriers.

Intellectual masculinity: Logical, intellectual, practical, or objective.

Interpersonal masculinity: Leader, dominating, independent, free, individualistic, or demanding.

Intersex: Formally termed hermaphrodites, individuals born with sex markers that may not be clearly recognized as male or female. These may include the genitals, gonads, chromosomes, and/or hormones.

Knowledge construction process: A technique in which teachers utilize activities that help students to understand, investigate, and determine how the implicit cultural assumptions, frames of references, perspectives, and biases of researchers and text-book writers influence the ways in which knowledge is constructed.

Latino: An individual of Mexican, Cuban, Puerto Rican, Central or South American descent or other Spanish origin or culture, regardless of race.

Lesbian: Romantic and sexual desires between females.

Masculinity: A term in American culture that specifically describes men and boys.

Moynihan Report: Also known as *The Negro Family: The Case for National Action*; written by sociologist Daniel Patrick Moynihan and released in 1965. Its focus was on the absence of the Black nuclear heterosexist family and how this absence might further impede economic and political equality for Black America. It also contributed to the deficit model thinking most educators have regarding the ability of students of color.

Multicultural education: An educational framework addressing cultural diversity and equity in schools by incorporating different cultural group membership emphasizing the interactions of race/ethnicity, gender, social class, and ability in students' lives.

Multiculturalism: The affirmation of multiple ethnic cultures, religious beliefs, and group identities without specifically promoting the values of one group over the other.

Native American: Indigenous people living within the United States. The term is also equivalent to American Indian; however, it is inclusive of all indigenous people on the North American continent.

Patriarchy: A social system where the father or the eldest male is the head of the household giving him control and authority over women and children. An institutionalized system of governance by males, as well as the disproportionate dominance of men in social or cultural systems.

Physical masculinity: Virile, athletic, strong, brave.

Post racial: A theoretical construct in which the United States is void of discrimination, prejudice, and racial preference. The election of Barack H. Obama as the first African American President of the United States of America has ushered in this theoretical position.

Prejudice reduction: A technique in which teachers facilitate activities and exercises through which students develop positive and democratic racial attitudes. It also helps students to understand how ethnic identity is influenced by the context of schooling and the attitudes and beliefs of dominant social groups.

Queer: Term reclaimed by the gay, lesbian, bisexual, and transgendered communities to refer to people who do not conform to culturally imposed norms of heterosexuality and traditional gender roles.

Questioning: A time or position where one re-assesses his or her sexual identity/orientation and/or gender identity.

Racial profiling: Law enforcement's use of an individual's race/ethnicity as a key factor in deciding to engage in enforcement. Term often utilized by scholars, policymakers, and community activists to question the disproportionate number of individuals of color who are under the custody and/or control of the criminal justice system.

Robber barons: A pejorative term for businessmen and bankers who dominated and controlled industries in the 19th century to amass huge personal fortunes and wealth, usually by unfair business practices. A resurgence of the term has occurred over the past 10 years.

Same-sex marriage: Also known as gay marriage, legally recognized marriage between two persons of the same biological sex or social gender. Same-sex marriage is a political, moral, civil rights, social, and religious issue in many nations.

Sexual masculinity: Sexually aggressive, experienced.

Social integration: Minority groups, particularly ethnic minorities, giving up their own cultural identities to assimilate into the dominant culture in order to gain access to the rights, privileges, and resources of that culture.

Special education: The education of students with special needs or accommodations by providing for the individual students' differences or needs; educational services designed to meet the challenges of students with physical disabilities, emotional/behavioral disorders, and developmental disorders. May also include services that are provided to students who are deemed academically talented or gifted.

Stonewall Riots: A series of spontaneous events and demonstrations against a police raid on June 28, 1969, at the Stonewall Pub and Bar in the Greenwich Village section of New York City. These events are the first in American history when individuals who identified as GLBT fought back against a system of government-sponsored enforcement that prosecuted non-conforming sexual identities. This is the defining event that marked the gay rights movement in the United States and around the world.

Straight: Term for someone who identifies as heterosexual-attracted to individuals of the opposite sex.

Transgender: Full range of expressions, identifications, and behaviors that challenge the binary gender system in society. The term serves as an umbrella that includes an array of differing identity categories such as transsexual, drag queen, drag king, cross-dresser, transgenderist, bi-gendered and several other identities.

Women's suffrage: The right of women to vote and to run for public office.

TECHNOLOGY, DIVERSITY, AND POPULAR CULTURE

Living in a Stockpile of Fear

The intersection of classes, cultures, and ethnic identities occur in public spaces (Robbins, 1993). Schools are public spaces that foster social solidarity, group identification, and community (Carlson & Apple, 1998). Depending upon the culture and climate of schools, these public spaces may also produce alienation for some students (Delpit, 1995; Ladson-Billings, 1997). Some schools are, in fact, sites of ongoing conflict and struggle for control (Gause, 2009; Weis, 1988). Public school administrators and teachers who seek to transform schools must operate from a position of understanding how critical pedagogy forces educators to critique the fundamental issues of power and its relationship to the greater societal forces that affect schools (Weis, 1988). Teaching and learning are a part of real life, and real life includes politics and people (Freire, 1970). Within the construct of real life is scripted and unscripted reality. This is the generation of The Millenials. They are the benefactors of the by-products of technology and science. This is the first generation to grow up in the digital age and with popular culture as the "background noise" of their very existence (Gause 2005b). There were many events of the last decade that caused this nation great pain; however, the economic crisis and the election of a man whose mother was a White academician from Kansas and whose father was a Kenyan reminded us as human beings to always remain hopeful. The United States of America continues to be a special jewel in the eyes of our global citizens because of the very historic moments that exist in our young history. On January 20, 2009, Barack Hussein Obama, the son of a Kenyan father and White mother from Kansas, was sworn in as the 44th President of the United States of America. The first time ever in the history of this land, a self-identified African American with a diverse background is the leader of this nation. The first 18 months of his presidency have been mired in double-digit unemployment, failed public policy, and national political unrest. The development of ultra-conservative grassroots movements like the Tea Party (Taxes Enough Already) have utilized the sting of racism and religious fundamentalism to further divide this nation into a binary construct—White religious conservative patriots versus "the other."

The media machines and mediums of a digital popular culture have turned this nation into a group of citizens living with a stockpile of fear. Families are living with a fear of foreclosure. Students are living with the fear of failing, fitting in, or being accepted. Schools are living with the fear of not meeting AYP. GLBT youth are living with the fear of being "outed." Undocumented workers are living with the fear of being caught, prosecuted, and/or deported. When will this nation of immigrants put our fears to rest and become benefactors of our differences? I thought we were on our way until a young Black United States Senator from Illinois with a multi-racial background like the very fabric of this nation took up residence in The White House on January 20, 2009. How could such a joyous occasion, one that appeared to unite these United States two years, turn out to be an event that causes a divide in this country greater than any event ever imaginable?

POST RACIAL AMERICA: GIVE ME A BREAK

The media, to describe discussions surrounding life in America after the election of Barack Obama, is using the term *post racial America*. The meaning: Race is no longer an issue in America. This is simply not true. Race does exist and, due to President Obama's election and current administration policies, race and racism has exacerbated. Believing that race is no longer a problem in the United States is an additional layer of burden for oppressed peoples who are fighting against their oppression while justifying that their oppression still exists. This is color-blind racism at its best. According to Bonilla-Silva (2007) in *Racism without Racists*, the four central frames to color-blind racism are abstract liberalism, naturalization, cultural racism, and minimization of racism. Bonilla-Silva describes the frames in the following way:

> …Abstract liberalism involves using ideas associated with political liberalism and economic liberalism in an abstract manner to explain racial matters… Naturalization …allows Whites to explain away racial phenomena by suggesting they are natural occurrences…cultural racism is a frame that relies on culturally based arguments…to explain the standing of minorities in society…minimization of racism…suggests discrimination is no longer a central factor affecting minorities' life chances." (pp. 28–29)

This significant milestone in America's history has forever changed the discourse with regard to diversity. In 2009, Sonia Maria Sotomayor became the first Hispanic justice appointed to the U.S. Supreme Court and only the third female. The media and events surrounding her appointment by the first African American President of the United States, Barack Obama, dominated much of our daily lives. This historic event was considered even greater than the one that took place 28 years before it: the appointment of Sandra Day O'Connor, the first female jurist to be appointed to the U.S. Supreme Court. Interestingly enough, the themes surrounding both of these appointments were equity and equality. However great the achievements and accomplishments of so many global citizens from diverse backgrounds, the close of the first decade and beginning of the second decade of the 21st century saw great economic depravity across the world.

The impact of the global economic crises and the series of earthquakes across the globe in 2010 will be recorded as events of catastrophic proportions. The earthquakes in Haiti and Chile reminded the global citizenry of our interdependence. As many nations across the globe continued to look to the United States for assistance to meet their needs, the "residuals of hope" that elected the first African American

President became "vapors of despair" as this nation engaged in conservative backlash. With rising unemployment and home foreclosure rates, increased numbers of those seeking unemployment, rising state taxes, increases in deficit speaking by our government, and the raging war over health care legislation, the first year of the second decade, 2010, has become the year of raging dissent, disgust, and disdained for our American life.

The outright disregard for individuals to engage in discourse that seeks to solve problems for the good of the whole while slandering and assassinating the characters of individuals who hold opposite views has become the norm. This is not democracy and it surely is not radical democracy; this is radicalism being fuelled under the auspices of "freedom of the press" by media conglomerates who find "corporatization of the media" and "free market systems" are the only answer to providing an objective "truth;" this machinery is being utilized by corporate interest groups not as a vehicle of inclusion but as a tool of exclusion. Many of you have been taught in schools and classrooms where bullying is acceptable. Attacking someone who looks different verbally and/or physically are a part of everyday schooling experiences.

Some of you have in your distant memories the possible impeachment of a sitting president, the fall of Enron, General Motors, Chrysler, Lehman Brothers, and AIG, and the greatest economic downturn since the Great Depression of the 1920's and 1930's. You are witnesses to the great disparity between the wealthy and the poor and the continuing destruction of our beloved planet in the name of corporate greed. Some of you received your formal K-12 education in re-segregated public schools fifty-five years after the landmark *Brown v. Board of Education* decision by the United States Supreme Court, which ended public school segregation. You have lived through the attack on the World Trade Center and two of the most horrific natural disasters of human record, the tsunami in Indonesia and Hurricane Katrina in the United States. You have witnessed the failure of the United States government to protect the basic human rights of her citizens, yet witnessed the election and inauguration of the first African American president of the United States, Barack H. Obama.

You are the Millenials. Your lives today are filled with blogs, MySpace, Facebook, chat rooms, texting, Tweets, the iPhone, and Google. You have the ability and capability to go Wi-Fi through virtual portals and entry points located in various locales across America. The Internet has become the vehicle for global socialization and information and, because of this, you have developed a new language to communicate to your friends via text messaging. Media outlets constantly bombard you with situations and circumstances that are detrimental to the human condition on a 24-hour basis.

The impact of war, famine, disease, and greed is a part of your daily news experience. The delivery of this information occurs so frequently I am greatly concerned for your emotional, mental, and physical health. I believe you have become anesthetized to it all. This generation is experiencing substance abuse at alarming rates, particularly as it relates to prescription drugs. You know individuals who are participating in the "underworld" economy and enjoy the sensationalism often presented by the media of this lifestyle. Members of this generation drink and drive at epidemic proportions and have no concern for falling behind their global peers in math and science.

All is not lost. I have faith and hope in this generation. This generation is the generation that will lead America into greatness. This generation will set new environmentally friendly policies and demand for the realization of international human rights. This generation, the Millenials, will insure everyone has universal health care and a living wage.

TEACHING THE MILLENIALS: A LIBERATORY PRACTICE

Teaching is a political as well as a liberatory practice. Our nation's freedom depends upon the development of enticing and exciting democratic learning communities where the pursuit of knowledge is the primary objective. Because American democracy is under a re-construction situated within globalization, evangelical fundamentalism, free market enterprise, and socio-cultural politics, the educational leader of today must be able to negotiate and navigate the often competing and conflicting forces of our democracy.

Teaching, learning, and leading democratically require constant participation with change. The purpose of higher education and K-12 public education is to provide opportunities and spaces for the global citizenry to engage in democratic practices for the public good. Democracy is an enacted daily practice whereby people interact and relate through daily personal, social, and professional routines with a primary focus on continuing the betterment of our humanity (Putnam, 1991; Carlson and Gause, 2007). This is the cause of education. In order to do this, higher education must prepare critical transformative leaders who are willing and able to draw upon culturally relevant, critical, and counter-normative pedagogies. I do this by infusing cultural studies in the leadership discourse of our educational leadership program (Gause, 2005b).

Indeed, hooks (2003) states:

We need mass-based political movements calling citizens of this nation to uphold democracy and the rights of everyone to be educated, and to work on behalf of ending domination in all its forms—to work for justice, changing our educational system so that schooling is not the site where students are indoctrinated to support imperialist White-supremacist capitalist patriarchy or any ideology, but rather where they learn to open their minds, to engage in rigorous study and to think critically. (p. xiii)

Critical change occurs with significant self-sacrifice, potential alienation, rejection, and costly consequences. As critical transformative educators, we must do justice to the larger social/public responsibility of our positions and roles, particularly in higher education. In (re) crafting the education of critical transformative leaders, we must demystify change, courage, and risk as we (re) imagine the language and fluency of multiple discourses in the rediscovery of democracy and social justice. This occurs in the development of the democratic classroom, which should be the hallmark of higher education. I evidence this by having students reflect upon one of hooks' (1994) most powerful statements regarding vulnerability and empowerment:

Any classroom that employs a holistic model of learning will also be a place where teachers grow, and are empowered by the process. That empowerment cannot happen if we refuse to be vulnerable while encouraging students to take risks. (p. 21)

This very act affronts the pedagogical challenges of seamless learning from K-20.

Critical transformative educational leaders who develop through the seamless K-20 educational system in the United States will facilitate the development of inviting, engaging and dynamic learning communities that: 1) transform the human condition, 2) unearth fallow ground, 3) interrogate and rupture the status quo, 4) question multiple political spaces critically, and 5) seek multiple epistemologies to re-create constructs that better serve our humanity. To further our thinking regarding the challenges of seamless learning from K-20, I call on all higher education faculties who actively serve in teacher education and/or educational leadership preparation programs around the country to (re) think the following by Gause (2005). He asserts:

> We are educating in a time of expanding globalization whose impact we witness via 24-hour digitally mediated discourse. How are schools and educational leaders keeping up with this global transformation? What type of impact does this transformation of schools from sites of democracy to "bedfellows" of consumerism have upon the school and much larger global community? How are the "souls" of schools affected? In the journey of school reform are educational leaders acknowledging that the "process of schooling" is filled with "cultural politics"? How are educational leadership programs preparing future school leaders? Are educational leadership preparation programs equipping schools' leaders for the "journey of the self" or for the "journey of the soul"? (p. 242)

As a former teacher, K-12 school administrator, principal and current faculty member in an educational leadership preparation program in the southeastern part of the United States, I work to co-create and decolonize democratic learning communities as a form of political activism. Critical transformative educational leaders must be able to utilize their positions to launch into the deep and ask hard questions, those to which there are no perfect answers.

Critical transformative educational leaders inspire and transform others to become more conscious of the human condition. Their leadership, teaching and practice are oriented towards a social vision and change empowering members of learning communities to generate ideas for problems with no current solutions. They regard resistance not as a form of protest, but as a standard for creating opportunities. Critical transformative educational leaders understand that it is their duty and responsibility to encourage other human beings, particularly those who are involved in the cause of education, to transform their environments, institutions, communities, neighbourhoods, and schools into arenas of social justice. They know they have a responsibility in transforming those in which they come in contact into advocates of radical democracy and leaders for equity and justice. Together we must face the struggle of educating our citizenry with nobility and commitment for together in the struggle, we are one.

The following section of this chapter contains my personal thoughts and strategies with activities to engage. This section could be utilized for students or adults.

KEYS FOR SUCCESSFUL STUDENTS/INDIVIDUALS

Answer the following two questions:

What are the things that I like to do and I find important?

What are my dreams/aspirations and what will it take to make them come true?

Creating successful learning experiences will require individuals to do the following:

Be prepared to achieve the impossible regardless of conditions and/or circumstances.

These are very difficult times for you as a student and youth. You have never seen an economic crisis of this nature nor did you ever think one could exist. You never thought there would be so many wars across the globe. You never thought you would have to leave your house, live with neighbors, live with other family members and/or strangers. You had some perspective of safety and a few things provided for you. These are tough times, but you will get through them. You must do your best and strive for excellence in all that you do.

List seven things that could help you do your best at school and at home:

1.

2.

3.

4.

5.

6.

7.

Integrity is your moral compass.

If you are going to be a part of the crowd, be the leader and lead with integrity. Earn your way through school by doing your best with all of the power that lies within you. Complete all assignments on time and with integrity. Do not settle for mediocrity and understand that your participation in the educational process is not a sport or extra-curricular activity, it is your job!

You exist in body, mind, and spirit; therefore, cultivate and nurture every aspect of your being.

To achieve greatness, you must cultivate and nurture every part of your being. In order to be successful you must do the following:

Exercise your body daily.
Exercise your mind daily.
Practice your faith daily.
Eat a well-balanced meal.
Read daily.
Study daily.
Develop a plan with goals and objectives.
Execute your plan.
Monitor and adjust your plan for success.
Listen intently to your elders for wisdom and for instruction from adults.

Answer the following question:

What do I want to become and/or do with my life?

List five goals you have for yourself to complete over the next 12 months:

1.

2.

3.

4.

5.

Envision where you want to go and what you want to achieve in life and then focus all of your energy towards the outcomes.

Whatever goal and/or life plan you have for yourself, you must focus all of your energies on completing this plan. In order for this plan to come to pass, it must be a plan of good and not evil and one that is not selfish or self-centered. It should be a plan designed to provide enough resources for a great life; however, it should not take advantage others nor allow for you to attain your goal at the expense of others.

Honesty, integrity, truth, justice, and respect coupled with hard work, dedication, compassion, and love will determine your success, not the amount of money you earn.

Money has nothing to do with success. Success is measured by how much you give to others and the impact you have on the communities which you inhabit. Success is about making the world a better place for EVERYONE!

Nothing in life is fair; however, you have the power to make it "just."

Life is not fair! It will never be fair! There will be pain, heartache, and challenges; however; you have the power to make life JUST! Decide on treating everyone with care and respect, regardless of how they treat you and seek to be just in the decisions you make so that everyone benefits and no one walks away feeling like a loser.

A change in your behavior is the only thing that will change your outcome.

If you want to see a change in the outcomes and events in your life, you must change your behavior. It takes 30 days to develop a healthy habit, but nearly a lifetime to break a bad one. Develop healthy habits of mind and heart and exercise them daily.

List three bad habits you will work on eliminating over the next two weeks:

1.

2.

3.

List five good/healthy habits you will develop and maintain over the next two weeks:

1.

2.

3.

4.

5.

Commitment to your dreams and goals will get you closer to achieving them then your talent alone.

Goal attainment is more about commitment than talent. Talent is only a small part of the equation. This is the equation for success: $2C + T = S$. It takes double the Commitment plus Talent to achieve Success. You must stick to what you believe and work hard at realizing your dreams. It can be done but not without great cost and sacrifice.

Transform your community by engaging in volunteerism and community service.

Everything we have in our society came at the price of blood, sweat, and tears. Volunteering and engaging in community service is your return on the investment many have made in you and your success. You owe your community and those who are a part of it for the opportunity to live, to work, and to pursue your education. GIVE BACK! It's not only the right thing to do; it is your responsibility as a citizen of this humanity.

Let go of old hurt, pain, and regret: They only serve as stumbling blocks towards achieving your destiny.

Forgive those who wrong you and ask forgiveness from those you have wronged. Life is a precious gift and the loss of life can be traumatic. It is better to live in peace and harmony then in regret.

List two people you will forgive right now and let them know you have forgiven them.

1.

2.

Conflict is a natural occurring phenomenon, how you deal with conflict will be the anomaly.

There will be conflict in your life. This is a part of the Circle of Life. How you deal with conflict will determine your character. Be kind, but firm, caring but strong, and affirming but resilient. These are the tests of your character. Do not bully, become hostile, seek to sabotage or assassinate someone's character.
Listen before speaking, and then decide if what you have to say is important enough to share with everyone.

We live in a time in which everyone is talking to someone. We are doing a lot of talking but very little listening. We should reduce the amount of time we talk by doubling the amount of time we listen. Listen not just to speech, but to the environment. Many of life's lessons can be heard in nature.

Treat your siblings with love and respect, because one day they may be your employer.

Brothers and sisters, your siblings, may often get on your nerves. You may have a bad relationship with one or more of them; however, be kind because one day they could be your employer. I know this can be difficult, but take time to get to know your siblings as individuals so, when you become adults, fond memories of your childhood will exist. Respect your siblings like adults and don't live in the past by reminding them of stuff that happened in childhood.

Limit the amount of time you spend in the virtual world on social networking sites.

Spend less time in the virtual world and more time in physical contact with people. The spirit of our humanity is only synergistic when human beings are in physical contact with one another. Technology has become a tool that maintains separation. It should be a tool to bring us together virtually and physically.

Volunteer your time and a portion of your earnings once a month to a charity that aid the needy.

Giving to charity is an important part of our humanity. It teaches us how to share our resources and it provides opportunities for expressing gratefulness and gratitude. Through your synagogue, temple, church, and/or local agency, give back to your community. Serving those in your community is indeed noble. Serving humanity is indeed greatness.

List three places you will volunteer sometime to the next 2 months:

1.

2.

3.

You are closer to greatness than you think.

Do not quit when times are the most difficult, because greatness is close by. If you truly believe you have given it all you have got and you have done your best, then complete that path with dignity and respect and move on to the next path.

Your knowledge, skills, and dispositions (attitudes) serve as the foundation to your academic success.

School is a place for inquiry, knowledge production, and knowledge attainment. As you learn new skills, they build upon others previously learned. The process of acquiring knowledge and producing knowledge is two sides of the same coin. Your attitude while gaining and sharing knowledge serves as the gatekeeper to gaining more and sharing more. If you want to success academically, then sharpen your skills, gain more knowledge, and have a great attitude in the process.

Answer the following question:

What are some things you can do to sharpen your skills and gain more knowledge?

Perseverance is the key to overcoming all of life's challenges.

The only way to overcome the pain, heartache, and challenges of life is to persevere. Life will continue to present opportunities and challenges for victory or defeat. It is up to you how you will engage. Don't give up or give in if you want to experience success and build your character. You must keep fighting. Those who stay in the fight will ultimately win. You must challenge yourself to gain greater strength for the fight before you. Endure life's challenges and you will be rewarded.

List three ways in which you will challenge yourself:

1.

2.

3.

Honor your parents, your teachers, your friends, your neighbors, and yourself.

There is no cost to HONOR someone. Be good to those around you and in your communities and by doing so you bring great HONOR to yourself.

List three ways in which you will show honor to those who take care of you:

1.

2.

3.

Just because you can does not mean you always should.

Do not do something just because you can. Many are imprisoned, incapacitated, and entombed because they did something just because they could. It is better to be cautious and advantageous than to be foolish and reckless. Opportunities will always come your way; however, it is important to choose wisely and carefully those in which you will engage.

Acknowledge your God-given gifts, talents, and knowledge by utilizing them for good and not evil.

Seek to do what is right at all times and forsake all that is evil. Your knowledge, gifts, and talents were granted to you to transform your community and to be independent. They are not designed for the trappings of selfishness. The talents, gifts, and knowledge placed within you by the Divine Creator should be utilized for the good of the community and not selfish gain.

List seven of your talents:

1.

2.

3.

4.

5.

6.

7.

Determine to be the best and the brightest in all aspects of your life and share that belief with everyone.

Challenging and loving yourself for who you are is the first key to being the best and brightest. What you do for those who are around you will speak to the fulfilment of your life. Developing and maintaining a positive attitude is the second key to being the best and brightest. By doing so, you realize failure is not an option and does not exist when you exercise your beliefs.
Answer the following question:

What are my beliefs and why are they important to me?

Dress for Success

Getting ahead in life requires a certain style of dress. You must dress for success and not based upon the elements of popular culture and fashion. Many of the outfits and styles you see are not designed for the workplace. If you load your closet up with the latest styles and fashions and do not have the proper attire for a job interview, you have just eliminated 80% of your success. Look your best, feel your best, and be your best.

GLOSSARY

Blogs: A type of interactive website or part of a website that provides regular entries of commentary, videos, news information, pictures, or other material on various topics.

Facebook: A social networking site launched in 2004 that connects users to other users. Individuals "friend" one another and this adds them to a listing for communication purposes. This site currently has 500 million worldwide users.

Google: A multi-national cloud company that operates internet search engines and data gathering systems for connectivity and profit. The term "Google" is a verb and noun; when you are searching for a something through this website, you "Google."

iPhone: An internet and multi-media enabled Smartphone that was designed and developed by Apple, Inc. The device contains digital media files including video, music, email, documents, and other mediums.

Millenials: The peer-oriented generation born between 1982 and 1995. The rise of instant digital communication via the Internet and connectivity via social networking sites, as well as the ability to self-produce and uplink video footage of themselves and friends, has increased the ease of this generation to facilitate communication via technology. They are consumers and producers of digital media unlike any other generation before them.

COLLABORATIVE ACTIVISM

Collectively Creating Change

Teaching, learning, and leading democratically require activism that is purposive, pragmatic, and transforming. The purpose of higher education and K-12 public education is to provide opportunities and spaces for the global citizenry to engage in democratic practices for the public good. Democracy is an enacted daily practice through which people interact and relate through personal, social, and professional routines with a primary focus on continuing the betterment of our humanity. This is the cause of education. To do this, higher education must prepare critical transformative leaders who are willing and able to draw upon culturally relevant, critical, and counter-normative pedagogies.

Critical change occurs with significant self-sacrifice, potential alienation, rejection, and costly consequences. As critical transformative educators, we must do justice to the larger social/public responsibility of our positions and roles, particularly in higher education. (Re) crafting how we view/see the world, educate global citizens, and produce knowledge will destroy the "veils of oppression." Demystifying change, being courageous, and taking extreme risks will aid us in (re) imagining the language and fluency of multiple discourses in the (re) discovery of democracy and social justice. Doing so will create spaces for the full expression of multiple identities that will not be viewed as deviant but affirmed as sources of beings. During a lecture at Harvard University in 1950, the anthropologist Margaret Mead noted:

> Teachers who are members of any group who are in a minority in their particular community will have to add in their own words that they are Negro teachers... as the case may be, redefining themselves against an image of woman who for most of the country is White, middle-class, middle-aged, and of Protestant background (1950: quoted in Foster, 1997, p. xvii).

As I survey the literature and reflect on the present educational statistical data in terms of the teaching force both K-12 and Higher Ed., as well as critically muse my research sites, I am astonished that a quote delivered sixty years ago continues to capture the condition of African American teachers and faculty of color presently. What will it take to bring about significant change? Do people understand there is a need for change? Those who are in the minority often do. However, I echo the concerns of Lindsey, Nuri-Robbins, & Terrell (1999): The primary barriers to this much-needed change are the presumption of entitlement and unawareness of the need to adapt. They state:

> People with a presumption of entitlement believe that they have acquired all the personal achievements and societal benefits they have accrued solely on their own merit and character and therefore don't feel a need to release or reorder any societal organizational perquisites they may have. Unawareness of

the need to adapt means failing to recognize the need to make personal and school changes in response to the diversity of people with whom one interacts simply because it never occurred that there was a problem. (p. 71)

The absence of the "voice" of the other is not a surprise when we realize that the American public educational system taught us to transmit the values and cultural norms of the dominant culture. Universities teach students the values of the dominant culture. These individuals become our nation's teachers who must teach students who enter their classrooms with cultural capital different from their own. Is it too late to realize this? Have we realized the importance of all "voices" or will those out on the margins continue to go unrecognized?

THE 21ST CENTURY UNIVERSITY

Transforming the university for the 21st century requires equity, diversity, and inclusiveness in all communities present within the university structure to include faculty, staff, and student body. There must be ethnic-linguistic minority faculty members in the faculty ranks of PWIs (predominantly White institutions) in order for their missions and visions to be realized. All forms of segregation, self-imposed or occurring due to power and privilege, must cease and desist. What I find interesting and sometimes difficult as a faculty member is having to defend the principles of *Brown* and many of the achievements gained during the civil rights movement, particularly with individuals who self-segregate. The systematic power of racism, segregation, and discrimination today in 2010 is a reality in higher education. The power of rank and privilege is often imposed on those without.

The latest population statistical data from the United States Census Bureau shows the southeastern part of the United States to have the fastest growing Hispanic population. There has also been a significant remigration of African Americans from Detroit, Chicago, and New York to the Southeast in search of better schools and affordable housing. This growth, however, also reveals that these individuals continue to experience higher rates of re-segregation based on class, gender, and race/ethnicity. In order to counteract this phenomenon, higher education institutions must diversify their faculty ranks.

Increasing the number of ethnic-minority faculty will improve the educational environment for all students. Diverse faculty will provide a rich learning experience for students. With numerous policy interventions (i.e., affirmative action) and legal precedents from the U.S. Supreme Court, which are presently being eroded, there have been some gains. What must faculty of color do in order to not be excluded? What roles must they fulfill to gain acceptance by colleagues whether White or of color? I utilize this space to share with you what has been done at one southeastern university to further the presence of faculty of color and to create a more inclusive learning community.

HISTORICAL OVERVIEW: INITIATIVES ENGAGED

Understanding the importance of a diverse faculty and the need for an effective recruitment and retention process for faculty from under-represented populations, a

special committee was established at Southern State University (pseudonym). This 8-member body was appointed with the following charges: —Review the triumphs and challenges of recruiting and retaining minority faculty and compare this data to peer institutions.
— Review promotion and tenure data of faculty by ethnicity including reviews at all levels.
— Query faculty of color to gain their perceptions regarding mentoring and support.
— Develop a set of recommendations to facilitate future work.

This subcommittee met several times, reviewed materials from multiple sources, accessed information from a several campus offices, attended conferences on the subject, and obtained an outside consultant to conduct fact-finding interviews. The consultant also surveyed faculty of color who departed the Southern State University.

Comparison Data: Peer Institutions

Data from the University Institutional Research office presented the percentages of ethnic minority faculty at designated peer institutions. Among the 11 institutions reporting these data, this university ranked 9th in overall minority representation, 3rd in Black non-Hispanic faculty, 9th (tied) in Native American faculty, 10th in Asian or Pacific Islander faculty, and 6th in Hispanic faculty. As you can see, the numbers were quite low; however, Southern State University felt it had made progress in recruiting and retaining minority faculty over the last decade. There were faculty and staff members who did not share the same perspective. They believed Southern State University had not made significant gains and continued to practice tokenism. Data provided by Human Resources revealed an increase in the percentage of ethnic minority tenure-track faculty between 1998 and 2007 at the ranks of Assistant Professor (from 7% to 22% of all tenure track Assistant Professors) and Associate Professor (from 7% to 13% of all tenured Associate Professors). Over the same time period, the percentage of professors remained constant at approximately 4% of all tenured professors.

Ten Year P & T Data by Ethnicity

The Office of the Provost provided promotion and tenure data to associate professor in the 10-year period 1997/98 to 2006/07. During this time frame, a total of 190 faculty were eligible for consideration, of which 163 (85.8%) were granted tenure and promotion. Of these, 138 (84.6%) were White, six (3.7%) were Black, 14 (8.6%) were Asian or Pacific Islander, and five (3.1%) were Hispanic. In the remaining 27 cases, (14.2%), tenure and promotion were not granted, either because the application was denied at any level or because the candidate elected not to come forward for consideration. There were seven cases (all White faculty) in which the candidate elected not to come forward. Of the remaining 20 cases which involved a denial of tenure, 17 (85%) were White and three (15%) were Asian; none were Black or Hispanic. Thus, the percentage of minority faculty among the successful and unsuccessful cases was almost exactly the same (15.4% and 15%, respectively).

Data provided did not indicate minority faculty were awarded tenure and promotion at Southern State University less often than their White colleagues. However, based upon anecdotal and informal communications, it appears faculty of color who may not be awarded tenure are counselled to depart after their 3rd year review or prior to going up for tenure. Many of these conversations are held in confidence.

MENTORING AND SUPPORTING FACULTY OF COLOR

A nationally recognized expert consultant in the area of diversity and faculty development was contracted to investigate how well Southern State University was doing in supporting and mentoring minority faculty. The subcommittee recognized the importance and value in gaining the experiences of current and former minority faculty as a viable data set for improving recruitment and retention. The consultant conducted a series of fact-finding interviews with current faculty and a web survey of former minority faculty. There were many responses from the interviewees. The following responses were extracted from reported comments directly relevant to faculty ethnicity:

- Minority faculty find White faculty, staff and students to be insensitive to and uninformed in issues relating to diversity.
- Minority faculty feel overwhelmed with committees and other service assignments, which they may be reluctant to refuse because of a sense of obligation to represent minority perspectives.
- Minority faculty feel, once hired, they are expected to be "just like" their majority colleagues, rather than expressing diverse point of views.
- Department culture is critical to minority faculty members' sense of satisfaction and belonging and the department head/chair plays a critical role in establishing that culture.
- Ethnic minorities are under-represented among faculty and administrators and feel isolated.

SPECIAL COMMITTEE RECOMMENDATIONS

The special committee, realizing their charge was limited to the recruitment and retention of ethnic minority faculty members, recognized the issue before them was embedded in a set of broader concerns regarding campus diversity. They believed the efforts to successfully recruit and retain ethnic minority faculty to Southern State University would depend on the degree to which senior administration is willing to address serious issues of diversity across campus. Therefore, the following ten recommendations were presented:

- Southern State U. should adopt a broad statement on diversity.
- Southern State University website should have a prominent diversity section.
- Organize annual workshops for department heads/chairs and search committee chairs to discuss strategies for more effective recruitment of minority faculty.
- Hire a Senior Executive Administrator to oversee diversity issues.
- Create an Office for Diversity.

— Include a diversity component in the faculty mentoring program.
— Include diversity as a more salient component of orientation for new faculty, staff, and students.
— Include diversity training as part of orientation for new department heads/chairs and university administrators.
— Extend invitations to minority scholars to campus so that faculty and students become aware of the wider range of disciplinary perspectives that are represented by diverse faculty.
— Each academic unit establish a mechanism to ensure issues of diversity receive sustained attention and action.

SPECIAL CAMPUS COUNCIL

The Special Campus Council was established in 2000 with the primary task of surveying the faculty, staff and student body every three years to gather longitudinal data regarding campus perceptions of diversity. The campus has been surveyed in 2000, 2003, 2005, and 2008. The Special Campus Council in 2008 partnered with Southern State's newly established Inclusive Task Force to update the data instrument so survey items would reflect specific issues surrounding diversity and inclusiveness. Surveys were distributed electronically to all faculty and staff and a random sample of students. Overall survey distribution and response rate is as follows:

Faculty: 370 of 1191 = 31.1% (95% confidence interval +/- 4.23)

Student: 591 of 3830 = 15.4% (95% confidence interval +/- 3.71)

Staff with e-mail: 685 of 2031 = 33.7% (95% confidence interval +/- 3.05)

Staff with e-mail and also others by hard copy: 703 of 2402 = 29.3% (95% confidence interval +/- 3.11)

Summary from Data

Faculty, staff, and students agree that diversity is represented in the Southern State University student body in numbers but not the quality. How are diverse populations embraced at Southern State University?

The data represented diversity in terms of ethnicity and international student populations, but not always in terms of sexual orientation, religious views, or political and ideological differences.

Faculty, staff, and students agree that efforts are lacking in terms of creating opportunities to strengthen and embrace diversity. They also agree that communication of such opportunities is poor.

RECOMMENDATIONS FROM THE DATA

Communication and Awareness

— Participants are not aware of Southern State University policies, procedures, or offices for ensuring a positive and supportive environment. University Web site creators and those who create publications should take this into account as new items are developed.

- Create a central site where community members can access information. Insure that those offices/groups that provide services or programming are regularly contributing to the site.
- Encourage and support open communication about issues relevant to the community.

Faculty Related Issues

- Place resources toward attracting several high profile senior faculty of color so that they can in turn help recruit and retain less seasoned faculty of color.
- Develop a university plan for recruiting, hiring, and retaining a diverse faculty and staff.
- Support alternative research and paths to promotion and tenure. Reward community engagement.

Further Education

- Black/White diversity was addressed but other racial groups are not as supported. Broaden the community's awareness of and support for other groups.
- Several community members suggested more diversity programs and training.

Group-specific Requests

- Consider how transfer students may be better engaged at Southern State University.
- Provide more resources for distance learners. They are a significant diverse population on Southern State's campus. Lack of religious diversity was mentioned several times.
- Consider Southern State University's holiday structures, calendars, and celebrations. Many activities may alienate non-Christian community members.
- Many community members noted that staff members who represent 85% of ethnic minorities on this campus are "unappreciated," "treated like second class citizens," "are not recognized adequately for their very hard work."

The following comment speaks to the importance of cultivating an inclusive campus community:

Faculty appointments are not as diverse as they need to be given the diversity of the Southern State University student population. I have seen little serious and creative effort going toward outreach to the increasing Hispanic population to cultivate and mentor them to attend college. Diversity programming at Southern State tends to be superficial and steer clear of social justice issues. Having many different types of people physically on the campus does not in itself mean that those people are engaging and learning from each other's differences. We fall short in this area of quality of engagement.

CAMPUS CLIMATE SURVEY RESPONDENT INCLUSIVE TASK FORCE

The findings of the Special Committee and the Special Campus Council's Campus Climate Survey suggested the need for a broader campus conversation about inclusiveness and diversity. Southern State's Chancellor and Provost are often stating publicly that Southern State is committed to supporting an inclusive community where there are visible, meaningful, and affirming representations of diversity present in the wider Southern State community at all university levels. In keeping with this commitment Southern State began a new initiative.

Beginning in August of 2008, the University Faculty Senate and Office of the Provost with support from the Office of the Chancellor, jointly established the Inclusive Task Force. This 26-member Task Force comprised of faculty, staff, student and community members were charged with the following:
— Conduct a campus climate assessment of the Southern State environment.
— Identify additional ways in which Southern State could become a more inclusive campus.
— Formulate a plan to better coordinate, communicate, and support all programs that contribute to campus inclusiveness.
— Develop a rationale and position description for a Director of Equity & Inclusion.
— Develop a Southern State-endorsed definition of an inclusive community that would be posted on the university website.
— In order to fulfill such an ambitious agenda, the task force was divided into the following 5 subgroups:
— Coordination & Communication of Inclusive Community Events
— Campus Climate Review & Assessment
— Data Surfacing Underrepresented Groups
— Southern State-Endorsed Definition of Diversity & Inclusiveness
— Position Description & Rationale for a Director of Diversity/Inclusivity

THE BEGINNING OF THE INITIATIVE

In an effort to successfully launch the Inclusive Task Force, the group collaborated with members of the Staff Senate and Faculty Senate to conduct an Open Mic Session. During this campus-wide forum, participants were given an opportunity to participate in a relationship-building exercise that provided the Task Force with information regarding the initiative. I provide you with the two central questions asked and some of the responses that were given at this forum.

What do you see as current barriers to Southern State being an inclusive community?
— Caste systems still in place (lack of opportunities for some members of campus to move into higher positions)
— Lack of education on campus re: diversity, similarities, & making the campus more inclusive
— Few GLBT staff and faculty members are out on campus
— Lack of accessibility of campus for all groups

- Lack of equal opportunities/benefits (e.g., no domestic partner benefits)
- Lack of time & space to build an inclusive community
- Fear of addressing issues related to diversity and creating a more inclusive community

What are your suggestions for ways to make Southern State a more inclusive community?
- Provide domestic partner benefits.
- Increase diversity across all parts of the campus.
- Make physical plant of campus accessible to everyone.
- Provide ongoing workshops on diversity and creating a more inclusive community.
- Make this issue a priority & provide time to build an inclusive campus.
- Allow staff to attend campus events without their having to use vacation time.

As a result of this Open Mic meeting, the Inclusive Task Force decided at their first business meeting to conduct focus-group panels with various under-represented groups on campus in order to hear directly from these individuals their perceptions regarding the level of inclusiveness at Southern State.

Over the two-year period following, ten panels were identified and conducted as part of this data gathering plan:
- GLBTIQQA* students
- Staff members
- International degree-seeking students
- Minority faculty members
- Minority students
- Male students
- Housekeeping staff
- Students with disabilities
- Adult students
- New faculty members

*Gay, Lesbian, Bisexual, Transgender, Intersex, Questioning, Queer, & Allied

A significant amount of data was surfaced from each group in response to the following four questions that were consistently posed to each panel:
- How inclusive is the Southern State University community?
- What contributes to Southern State University being an inclusive community?
- What are current barriers to Southern State University being a more inclusive community?
- What are your suggestions for ways Southern State University could become a more inclusive community?

The data were analyzed for themes. A second method used for gathering data from staff members of the university community was through 15 interviews that were conducted by sophomores involved in a writing- and speaking-intensive English course. The instructor of the course was a task force member and decided it would be a great action-research project for his students. The instructor/task force member coordinated these interviews, collected all student-generated data, analyzed and summarized the data for major themes from the interviews, and provided a report to the task force. All data from the focus group panels and student interviews were placed into data summary tables and included as a part of the final report submitted to university officials. Because of the large amount of data collected, I present to you a few snapshot responses from the minority faculty data-surfacing panel. The following data was obtained from 11 Southern State University minority (broadly defined) faculty members representing a wide variety of departments across the campus.

"A culture and history exist around framing diversity around gender; particularly around White women and placing them in leadership."

"Faculty in my department thinks I am a fornicator and I find that quite problematic."

"There are a number of Latino students who are dissatisfied with their classification by enrollment services as being Hispanic. They are being classified as Hispanic and do not like the classification. They would rather be classified as Latino, Chicano, or Mexican-American etc."

"Many Latino students are marking 'other' instead of Hispanic on demographic data forms. Which means we actually have more identified Latinos on campus than what the data shows."

"Southern State University is not inclusive at all, particularly with GLBT faculty."

"I am a South-Asian Lesbian who believes this community (Southern State University) has not reached out to the GLBT community."

"No support system for GLBT faculty."

"African Americans are promoted in leadership positions but are not allowed to stay."

"We have attended Latino events and many Latino students are dissatisfied with their experiences."

"Not enough tenured faculty of color, particularly black faculty."

"No same-sex partner benefits-gain them."

"People in leadership positions should engage in serious dialogue around retention of faculty members from under-represented groups."

–Establish a GLBT Center
–Establish an African American Center
–Establish a Latino Center

Key Question for Administration: What are the transformational institutional practices and policies that would create spaces for inclusiveness?

"Upper administration must take on the central apparatuses; which supports barriers in departments and schools. They must develop values that support inclusiveness and provide resources to insure things get done."

"Upper administration must also address the inconsistencies that occur with the tenure and promotion process."

"Review programs, opportunities, and events across the campus and support them, as well as communicate them across all channels."

STATUS OF TASK FORCE

At the conclusion of the 2008–2009 academic year, the Inclusive Task Force: 1) developed a broad definition statement on diversity and inclusiveness, 2) developed a plan for marketing and communicating all inclusive events across campus, 3) developed a rationale and job description for an executive staff level position, 4) conducted a campus climate assessment containing additional items focused on inclusiveness, and 5) conducted data-surfacing focus group panels with six targeted populations on campus. A final report with the following recommendations was presented to university administration:

- Re-establish the Inclusive Community Initiative-Task Force as the Chancellor's Advisory Committee on Equity, Diversity, and Inclusion.
- Secure office space for the Office of Equity and Inclusion.
- Identify budgetary resources to support the initiative.
- Identify graduate assistant to serve the initiative.
- Continue work on university-wide endorsement of the recommended inclusiveness definition.
- Fold the work of the Campus Special Council into the work of the Chancellor's Advisory Committee on Equity, Diversity, and Inclusion.
- Present proposed rationale and position description for the Vice Chancellor of Equity and Inclusion to targeted university community groups.

At the conclusion of the 2009–2010 academic year, the Inclusive Task Force recommended the following:

- Expansion of university support services to include GLBTIQQA (Gay, Lesbian, Bisexual, Transgender, Intersex, Queer, Questioning, and Allied) students, faculty, & staff.
- Expansion of retention & recognition efforts regarding students, faculty, & staff with a particular focus initially on staff members.
- Review and revise hiring policies & practices to ensure greater diversity in administrative positions at Southern State University.

The Inclusive Task Force has recommended and received full support from the Chancellor to conduct three administrative planning sub-groups in 2011. This will allow data gathering and contributions from key members of the Southern State University community to further examine, delineate, and obtain full support for each initiative.

SUMMARY/CONCLUSION

We continue to move towards a more inclusive community by making strides in recruiting and retaining faculty of color through the promotion and tenure process. Through the various initiatives undertaken over the past three years, we have evidence that our efforts are paying off. At the beginning of this academic year, we saw an increase in the number of ethnic minority faculty recruited to Southern State University as well as an increase in the number of those promoted and tenured. The percentages of ethnic minority tenure-track faculty in 2009 are 29% for assistant professors, 16% for associate professors, and 9% for professors. Also at the beginning of this academic year, the Chancellor accepted the recommendations of the Inclusive Task Force and established the Office of Equity, Diversity and Inclusion with an office in the Chancellor's suite.

The multiple initiatives undertaken by Southern State University over the past three years are indicative of what it takes to successfully increase the recruitment and retention of minority faculty members. Support and commitment to this critical issue must take place at all university levels including administration, faculty, staff, and students. Higher education institutions must be willing to make a complete shift in policies, practices, and community climates that fully support and embrace the belief that diversity and inclusion at all levels strengthens the university for the 21st century.

A MESSAGE TO HIGHER EDUCATION

Educators who come to the academy in which I serve are searching for answers. These individuals struggle with how to implement local, state and Federal legislation, seek efficient and effective ways to provide optimal learning experiences for all members of the learning community, and strive to make sense of the dynamic cultures in which they work professionally. During this era of market competition, globalization, and educational accountability, the challenge of the academy is transforming those aspiring educational leaders who are concerned more with "the bottom line" into critically conscious democratic leaders who seek to develop free-thinking members of our society. Given the call for "principal executives," democratic education and freedom have been reduced to the ability to achieve academic standards and acquire material goods, wealth, and power without critiquing the consequences of inequity, greed, and inequality.

The national economic downturn, the last wave of horrific budget cuts, and the present political climate are adding to the hurdles for educators, particularly administrators, who must successfully educate students with less than adequate resources. These resources are not just monetary but human as well. The current socio-cultural political climate in the United States, the renewing of the Patriot Act, disaster relief or the lack thereof, terrorism and homeland security, the demonization of those in poverty, and the privatization of free public education forces me to ask the following central question:

What is the promise and purpose of an education from institutions of higher learning?

Higher education and K-12 public schooling has changed significantly within the past ten years. The advancement of the democratic promise of public education continues to be challenged by political and economic forces, which constrain the opportunities for America's citizenry to enhance the value of one's life by accessing public colleges and universities and by benefiting from a "free" public education. The work in which we do must engaged the communities in which we inhabit not as subjects to be researched, but as collaborators in the process of inquiry, if we seek to transform our humanity.

Public schools are the basic foundation for developing an informed citizenry, fully capable of self-governance. They are capable not because of the tools we provide, but because they arrive to school with a critical consciousness that allows them to question. It is up to us to enhance the skills of those we teach so they will be able to awaken that consciousness.

Given the promise of public education, I ask each of you to focus on the following questions:

– What are the pedagogical challenges of co-creating democratic spaces with practitioners to provide for seamless learning through the K-20 educational experience?

– How do we collaborate, (re) create, and (re) conceptualize institutions and systems of education into affirming, dynamic, and engaging learning communities that are anti-oppressive and inclusive?

As a creative educational leader who embodies education as praxis of freedom, my perspective of democracy is evidenced in my practice. I strive to co-create learning environments where all member-voices are given the opportunity to be heard, shared, and awakened. The dialogic encounter is central to (de) constructing and (re) constructing spaces for knowledge acquisition and development. In order for the citizens of the United States to continue to engage in "life, liberty and the pursuit of happiness," democracy must exist in institutions that encourage human beings to transform our environment, communities, neighborhoods, and schools into arenas where dialogue, discourse, and dissent are not silenced but celebrated.

The aforementioned should be the foci of K-20 public and private education in the United States. Instead of continuing to view public schools as sites of reform, we must transform the role, function, and purpose of schooling. Those of us who teach in colleges of education realize the importance of language and how it informs practice. Moving students from the language of reformation to transformation is often difficult and viewed as counter-productive; however, if schools are to be sites of democracy, this is the path of liberation. I encourage students to view themselves not as mere custodians of buildings of learning, but as proactive transformational leaders. Such a role involves understanding the schools culture and transforming custodial organizations into creative learning communities. This change requires transformational leadership that is creative, courageous, and visionary.

GLOSSARY

Dialogic: Continuing and ongoing conversations and responses by utilizing what has been said in the past and anticipating what will be stated in the future.

Peer institutions: Institutions that serve the same type of demographics, are approximately the same size, offer many of the same degrees and programs, and may or may not be located within the same region.

Race: As a socially constructed category of human difference and division. Although the boundaries and meanings have changed over time, the category of race, however, is always a mechanism for the unequal distribution and allocation of social goods and status.

Transformation: Dynamic change process by adapting to external and internal forces.

Transformational leadership: An approach to leadership that creates significant change in followers that is positive and valuable. The goal of this style of leadership is to turn followers into leaders.

Veils of oppression: A social distancing of those impoverished and maintenance cultural identities with regard to social status.

THEORIZING IDENTITIES

Educators of Color–How Do We Feel?

Creating professional learning communities that attract qualified faculty members, regardless of race, should be the goal of any institution of higher education. For predominantly White institutions committed to creating racially inclusive professional learning communities, constructing communities that sustain faculty of color requires an examination of the institution's culture, as well as ways in which the institution might exclude (whether explicitly or implicitly). It also requires recognition of the roles faculty of color might be asked to fulfill. These roles may not be congruent with the faculty member's perspective on gaining tenure. The roles also might be subjugating and subversive. Most important, it demands a "truth telling" process. This truth telling will require White faculty and White administrators to attentively listen to their colleagues of color. It will also require faculty of color to listen attentively to their White colleagues and both groups to engage in dialogue regarding how the institutional culture of the university contributes to and/or impedes the development of sustainable, inclusive democratic learning communities.

The absence of faculty of color at PWIs and the inability of PWIs to create and sustain racially diverse professional communities continues to be debated in academic and professional communities, particularly by scholars of color. Ultimately, the creation of racially diverse professional learning communities at PWIs requires a transformation of the institutional culture. A transformation of this type and at this level, regardless of institution, requires thoughtful and proactive leadership.

Herein I briefly examine the roles and expectations of faculty of color at PWIs using auto-ethnographic and theoretical lenses. I utilize my lived experiences, the lived experiences of other faculty of color at PWIs, and the typology developed by Roseboro & Gause (2009) to bring perspective regarding how faculty of color most often must navigate and negotiate (overt and/or covert) oppressive institutional structures and practices. The typology presented by Roseboro & Gause is re-articulation and synthesis of what has already been critiqued, discussed, and deconstructed among faculty of color. They recognize that a typology by its very nature does not essentialize experiences nor do they presume all faculty of color share the same beliefs. I concur with their presuppositions. Understanding this, what White people often assume is that all people of color identify with one another across some predetermined psychological bond. This unto itself is troubling and comes out of White privilege. I do believe that being oppressed, othered, or raced generates similar interpretive historically contextualized frameworks that implicate how people respond and act.

Positionality matters because the presence of faculty of color at PWIs holds both symbolic and real significance. It calls into question racist presumptions that faculty of color do not belong at PWIs and in such positions. The situatedness of faculty of color at PWIs has been explained in a number of ways, particularly in deficit discourses. Most researchers explain the low numbers of faculty of color in the following ways: 1) institutional structures make it more difficult for faculty of color to get tenure; 2) racist attitudes and practices make the working environment intolerable; 3) feelings of isolation and alienation stem from being the only or one of few people of color, 4) the minority Ph.D. candidate pool is low, and 5) there is a failure to appreciate scholarship on issues related to race written by faculty of color. Ultimately, there is no one explanation that exists to explain why there are so few faculty of color teaching at PWIs, particularly in tenure-track lines.

Various researchers point to the ways in which faculty of color are marginalized, erased, silenced, or ignored once hired at PWIs and how they are simultaneously hypervisible and invisible, seen yet not heard. Stanley (2006) sums up the discursive constructs of faculty of color at PWIs: "multiple marginality, otherness, living in two worlds, the academy's new cast, silenced voices, ivy halls and glass walls, individual survivors or institutional transformers, from border to center" (p. 3). While this list is not exhaustive, it does capture the core of what has been written about faculty of color at PWIs.

Faculty members of color are subjects (see Freire, 1970) and agents who exercise power in complicated ways. While they work within pre-existing hegemonic structures, such structures are not completely closed spaces; I believe there is always space for contestation and change. As a faculty member of color, I recognize that I enter and resist these spaces with confidence, intellectual capability and stamina, but also weariness. I do not enter these spaces assuming I must fulfill the roles assigned to or expected of me. Instead, I enter with caution and boldness, knowing that I am under the gaze and any decision that I make may irrevocably alter my professional life and the lives of other faculty of color.

Roseboro & Gause (2009) have performed or witnessed other faculty of color enacting the following roles: Suspect, Diversity Witness, Affirmative Action Statistic, Contract Worker, Code Breaker, and Informant. As an African American male academician, many of the critical perspectives regarding the intersections of race, class, and gender affront the White Southern Christian values many of my students' hold near and dear. The expectation is for me to operate out of false civility and behave as if these values should not be critiqued and/or interrogated, but honored and celebrated regardless of how they assault the plurality of values students bring into public schools and spaces daily. When coupled with my being a faculty of member of color, regardless of credentials, ideological orientation and instructional style, my students at times implicitly and explicitly challenge my professorial authority, scholarship, intellect, and political agenda. After speaking truth to power in many of our dialogic encounters, I have often heard students call me "the angry Black man" or "Dr. Thug." I find it interesting how they construct my passion for the subject and fiery delivery style as a place of subjugation. Given the atrocities occurring in public education in our nation today, we should all be angered to action. In order to transform schools, we must hold our students accountable. We do this by shifting them from a traditionalist view of education and democracy to one that is radical and transformative. We can do this by promoting environments that require students to engage in independent thinking and motivate them to take ownership of their learning process and by providing opportunities for rigorous intellectual study and committed activism that moves beyond arriving at the "right" answers. This requires critical change in how we teach in elementary, secondary, and higher education.

Teaching is a political as well as a liberatory practice. Our nation's freedom depends upon the development of enticing and exciting democratic learning communities where the pursuit of knowledge is the primary objective. Because American democracy is under a re-construction situated within globalization, evangelical fundamentalism, free market enterprise, and socio-cultural politics, the educational leader of today must be able to negotiate and navigate the often competing and conflicting forces of our democracy. Teaching, learning, and leading democratically require constant participation with change. The purpose of higher education and K-12 public education is to provide opportunities and spaces for the global citizenry to engage in democratic practices for the public good.

Critical transformative educational leaders who develop through the seamless K-20 educational system in the United States will facilitate the development of inviting, engaging and dynamic learning communities that: 1) transform the human condition, 2) unearth fallow ground, 3) interrogate and rupture the status quo, 4) question multiple political spaces critically, and 5) seek multiple epistemologies to re-create constructs that better serve our humanity. To further our thinking regarding the challenges of seamless learning from K-20, I call on all higher education faculty members who actively serve in teacher education and/or educational leadership preparation programs around the country to (re) think the following:

- We are educating in a time of expanding globalization whose impact we witness via 24-hour digitally mediated discourse.
- How are schools and educational leaders keeping up with this global transformation?
- What type of impact does this transformation of schools from sites of democracy to "bedfellows" of consumerism have upon our society and the global community?
- How are colleges and universities preparing today's digital generation?

As a critical transformative educational leader, I inspire and transform others to become more conscious of the human condition. My teaching and practice is oriented toward social vision and change, not simply or only organizational goals. My teaching is a form of protest and collaborative activism.

One of the biggest disappointments I face as an educator is having my soul and spirit ripped right out of my work. As an educator, I am faced with continually encouraging students, educators, and parents in the midst of harsh realities—funding shortages, accountability, and testing challenges, in addition to tightening legislative policies, which squeeze the life out of our optimism on a daily basis. Our lives today are filled with the availability of global news 24 hours a day. The media is filled with situations and circumstances, which are detrimental to the human condition, such as war, famine, disease, and greed. Do we want to continue on this self-destructive path? Education was once presented as "the great equalizer." However, the ability to make large sums of money at an alarming rate and at the expense of others seems to dominate. It's become more and more about "the Benjamins" and less and less about education. The world of entertainment in its many facets has grown into a multi-trillion dollar business while education has taken the back seat. Many cities in the United States are striving to build new football, basketball, and baseball stadiums instead of building new infrastructure and school facilities. This perspective has communicated and created a generation of students who believe the desires of the individual are more important than group success. With that in mind, we have seen an increase in the "underworld" economy. Students are becoming substance abusers at alarming rates. Recreational drugs are more prevalent in high schools today than textbooks. The War on Drugs has been replaced with The War on Terrorism, which is indeed a political act because America was losing the War on Drugs anyway. The representations of Black masculinity by popular culture continue to give young Black men a false construction of who they are. By drawing on deeply felt moral panics about crime, violence, gangs, and drugs, numerous Black entertainers, namely athletes and rap artists, have rewritten the historic tropes of Black masculinity from provider and protector to pusher and pimp.

As a researcher and scholar viewing Hip Hop, I find that Hip Hop is the first art form where the Black man has pimped himself before the White man beat him to it. This corrosive nihilistic construction of maleness reifies notions of (hyper) sexuality, insensitivity, and criminality, which serve as the new tropes of fascination and fear for the dominant culture. It becomes a "veil" of Black masculinity. The cultural effects of these images are as complex as they are troubling. The complex cluster of self-representations embodied in images of the Black male as rap artist, athlete, and movie star is complicit in racist depictions of Black males as incompetent, over-sexed, and uncivil—ultimately a perceived threat to middle class notions of White womanhood, family, and patriotism. Self-representations of Black male youth who construct their identities based upon these mediated images rely upon definitions of manhood that are deeply dependent on traditional notions of heterosexuality, authenticity, and sexism. Black heterosexual male youth who employ these representations see themselves as soldiers in a war for their own place in American society.

These soldiers believe, in doing battle, they must threaten and challenge the White man's (liberal and conservative) conceptions of public civility, private morality, and individual responsibility. Through this performative act of Black masculinity, these youth become casualties of their own war.

The fact remains that mainstream America is ignorant about education that is culturally relevant and the impact of that education on today's classrooms. In order to address the ignorance of mainstream America, we must answer the following questions:

1. What must school districts do to respond to this pervasive culture (any culture that is not the dominant)?
2. What is the role of leadership how must it change and/or adapt?
3. What is the role of teacher preparation and educational leadership programs in universities in this process?

MY PERSPECTIVE: C. P. GAUSE, PH.D

I entered the field of education after completing degrees in Business and Religious Studies and have spent the past eighteen years in the field of education. I started my first teaching assignment in the very high school from which I graduated as a long-term substitute while completing my Master's in Elementary Education. I soon realized the youth of the 1990s had very different issues to negotiate than the youth of the 1970s and 1980s. Upon completing my Master's degree, I remained in the school district in which I received my public education, as a fifth grade teacher.

I was the only male beside the principal and custodian in an urban school where there was only one White student. That student was in my class and he did not see himself in terms of Whiteness, which worried his mother. I learned a lot from my first class about why things are the way they are, but didn't have to be, and I began to see myself as an agent of and for change. I eventually became an assistant principal of a majority-minority elementary school in a district that was under desegregation consent decree before becoming principal of a rural school where students identified themselves as Black or multiracial. All the White students attended private schools.

Still looking for new ways of knowing, I entered a Ph.D. program with many questions concerning the marginalization of African Americans, particularly African American males and how educators perceive them. During the coursework, I was exposed to scholars who critiqued schools in terms of the power differential. I was introduced to critical pedagogy, critical race theory, and post-modernism. I realized how I felt about what we were doing to children was not far off the mark and, since then, discovered that the 20th century, the period of my youth, is vastly different from the 21st century digital age.

Historically, members of our society, particularly African Americans, viewed education as the most accessible means for achieving social, political, economic, and cultural liberation in the United States. My parents often preached to my siblings and me, in order to make it, you need to get a good education. My father still believes this to some degree without giving any regard to systemic issues of oppression and racism. He was taught to believe in meritocracy. As a former P-12 educator, I witnessed the many barriers of access and equity to those who did not understand how to navigate and negotiate school politics. I utilize my position as a teacher, scholar, researcher, cultural critic, and collaborative activist to negotiate these barriers to create affirming, engaging, and dynamic successful learning communities for all members regardless of difference.

GLOSSARY

Affirmative action statistic: Race-based assignments in public schools were dismissed by the U.S. Supreme Court; however, affirmative action in higher education remains a possibility. Many institutions of higher education continue to adopt and maintain diversity goals as a part of their mission. These cases are not directly applicable to faculty and staff; however, they do hold specific implications for universities and their hiring processes. As purported sites of democracy, the purpose of higher education is to educate students for life in civic society.

Black masculinity: A social construction of physical, cultural, political, emotional, and performative behaviors of biologically sexed males whose lineages are connected to the continent of Africa with an appropriation of slavery as the historical context.

A construct of raced/sexualized (re) presentations of Black male performance within popular culture.

Code breaker: At times, academics of color translate the "world of color" to White people who may misinterpret, misuse, or misappropriate. Such interpreting/translating does not come without specific consequences. It places the interpreter/translator between worlds, knowing that neither can fully be home.

Collaborative activism: An approach to education that is rooted in democracy. It unites educators, teachers, students, learners, parents, and community members in the process of raising consciousness and rupturing the status quo in order to socially deconstruct, politically transform, and create systemic change in oppressive institutions and organizations.

Contract worker: We will never quite be a part of the dominant culture of the institution, we will always function as contract workers because we do not hold, by cultural or racial virtue, a permanent place at the institution; we feel that we are "on loan" until we become too militant, race(y), or unpredictable.

Diversity witness: We often find ourselves assigned to diversity committees or projects, selected to other committees as the minority representative, or asked to facilitate diversity discussions. Hence, we find ourselves, whether "qualified" or not, speaking to the historical evolution of race relations in the United States.

Hip hop: Intense body culture with expressions in dance, voice, and gestures; highly vocal culture with rap music providing its voice and sound; a highly visual culture, creating its distinctive art form from graffiti, urban streets as well as fashion.

Informant: We are primarily speaking and listening in different voices. There are times, however, when we are expressly expected to provide critical information about one group's intentions and motivations.

Meritocracy: A system whereby roles and/or responsibilities are bestowed upon an individual based upon how hard they work and/or their intellectual ability.

PWIs: Predominantly White institutions, this term and/or acronym is often utilized to denote institutions of higher education who currently and/or historically have had a majority of White student populations.

Rap: A genre of music that initially articulated the experiences and conditions of African-Americans living in a spectrum of marginalized situations ranging from racial stereotyping and stigmatizing to struggling for survival in violent ghetto conditions. Currently commodified, rap is a performance of lyrics with music voice-overs.

Suspect: As suspect, every interaction in the classroom potentially becomes a site of contestation in which we, the instructors of color, strike a responsive posture predicated upon the implicit defense of our race. This defensive racial posture embeds itself within student–teacher situations which already harbor the potential for conflict (e.g., discussions about grades or classroom policies). If suspect, faculty members of color cannot enter public conversations or professional learning communities without having to compensate for their raced inferiority.

RESOURCES AND REFERENCES

The following case study is presented to engage the reader in practical application of theories, ideologies, and information presented in this text.

CASE STUDY 1: LIFE AND TIMES AT LINCOLN JUNIOR-SENIOR HIGH

This case study is designed to challenge the beliefs, values, and ideologies of under-graduate and graduate students in teacher preparation and higher education pre-paration programs regarding social justice and democratic education. This case is designed to assist students in developing the knowledge, skills, and dispositions to navigate the micro-political environments that exist in learning communities. This case navigates the multiple socio-cultural and political issues a superintendent or educational leader might experience regarding demographic and cultural change. The case is multi-layered and can be used in a variety of courses.

Case Narrative

Overview—The Community Lincoln Independent School District (LISD) is located in the town of Lincolnville, which happens to be 70 miles from a major urban center in the southeastern part of the United States. The city of Lincolnville continues to undergo demographic change. The city has increased from 25,000 residents to more than 185,000 residents within the past 15 years and has experienced a significant increase in its immigrant population, particularly within the Hispanic and Middle Eastern communities. Affordable housing is becoming more prevalent in the town of Lincolnville, as well as a new proliferation of government-subsidized housing.

The LISD consists of four elementary schools, two middle schools, one junior–senior high school, one comprehensive high school, and one early college program housed at Lincolnville Community and Technical College.

Lincoln Junior and Senior High Schools merged into one school 3 years ago. Both schools are located geographically on the same site. The citizens of Lincolnville support their public schools via local property taxes. A school tax levy has not passed within the last five years because of the loss of several textile-based manufacturing jobs and the closing of one of the Big Three auto makers' plants located in the north-east section of Lincolnville. Given the economic downturn over the past 5 years and the shift in demographics, the parent community continues to remain very active. In its earlier history, the LISD was recognized both statewide and nationally for its outstanding athletic and academic programs. The district has not been recognized for the past three years, and many believe it is due to the town's changing demo-graphics. The mayor and town council are concerned about how this may affect attracting local businesses to the town of Lincolnville and have called on the school board for changes.

The Lincoln Independent School Board is comprised of seven members. Five members are European American including three men and two women. One board member is an African American male and the other is a Hispanic female. All members of the board have maintained their residences and businesses within the Lincolnville community for more than 20 years. The board members decided to name an "outsider" as the superintendent, believing this would provide a platform for a renewed commitment to the district's recently adopted vision, "Striving, Achieving, Excelling: 100% of Lincoln students at/or above grade level by 2010." At his or her appointment, the student reader was reminded that his or her goal as the new superintendent was to bring Lincoln Junior–Senior High School and the LISD to national prominence.

Superintendent Prior to the student reader's appointment as superintendent, Dr. Carlos Smith led the district. Under his leadership, LISD experienced 15 years of great academic and athletic growth. He was considered Lincoln's greatest superintendent and one of the state's most progressive educators. He was at the forefront of social justice and championed the causes of equality and equity for all. He was responsible for hiring Dr. Leslie Jones, the state's principal of the year, back to LISD where she began her career. He did so because she embodied the very ideas he championed. Prior to her returning, Dr. Jones was principal extraordinaire at Starmount High School, located 30 miles east of LISD. She gained a national reputation for her commitment to education and for leading one of the nation's top high schools. Under her leadership, Starmount High received the U.S. Department of Education's Presidential High School of Excellence award.

Also during this time, under the direction of Dr. Smith, the school board passed the following Discrimination-Free Zone Policy:

It is the policy of the LISD to maintain a learning environment that is free from harassment, bullying, and discrimination. This includes but is not limited to harassment, bullying, and discrimination based on an individual's real or perceived race, color, sex, religion, creed, political beliefs, age, national origin, linguistic and language differences, sexual orientation, gender identity/ expression, socioeconomic status, height, weight, physical characteristics, marital status, parental status, or disability. The Board prohibits any and all forms of harassment because of those differences. It shall be a violation of this policy for any student, teacher, administrator, or other school personnel to harass, bully, or discriminate against any person based on any of the differences listed above. It shall also be a violation of this policy for any teacher, administrator, or other school personnel to tolerate such harassment, bullying, or discrimination of any person by a student, teacher, administrator, other school personnel, or by any third parties subject to supervision and control of the LISD (Guilford County Schools, 2006).

Many members within the district's communities viewed these acts by Dr. Smith as legacy builders. Dr. Smith retired after 35 years in the field of education and relocated to the Pacific Northwest. Prior to his departure, he lobbied the school board to name Dr. Jones as Lincoln's next superintendent.

Principal. Dr. Jones began her teaching career at Lincoln Junior–Senior High School and has served in various teaching and administrative positions in neighboring school districts for the past 20 years. She has spent the last 4 years as the principal and just recently announced her plans to leave at the end of this school term to become the superintendent of a neighboring school district. The pressures of serving as the principal of Lincoln were beginning to show, and it had nothing to do with the school and the students. Dr. Jones believes, after providing stability for the past three years, it is time for her to retire. She has recommended Mr. T. Jorge Azul for the principalship. Mr. Azul has served as a biology teacher and girl's varsity soccer coach at Lincoln. He is now completing his fourth year as assistant principal at Lincoln. Dr. Jones believes Mr. Azul provides agency for all students. She also believes Mr. Azul's transformational leadership style would bring about the changes needed at Lincoln.

Assistant Principal. For the past 8 years, Mr. Azul, known to the students as "Coach TJ," has been a Lincoln faculty member. He is originally from the Dominican Republic and speaks Spanish, French, and English fluently. Mr. Azul was adopted when he was 11 years old by two professors doing research in the Dominican Republic. He became a U.S. citizen on his 18th birthday. He received his Bachelor of Science degree in biology from an Ivy League school and decided to be a teacher instead of a doctor. He received his Master of Arts in School Administration from a major research university in the Midwest and moved to Lincoln when his parents retired from higher education.

Mr. Azul started teaching at Lincoln when the demographics began to change. He taught biology for four years and coached the girl's varsity soccer team to three state championships. Mr. Azul is widely known by members of the Hispanic community as "El Profesor." He is considered a local hero after the news media videotaped him bringing about a truce in one of the most violent gang wars in Lincoln to date. He gave up coaching to become the assistant principal four years ago because he wanted to make a difference. Mr. Azul is currently enrolled in a Ph.D. program at the local state university that emphasizes educational leadership and social justice.

The Issues

Demographics. Lincoln is comprised of 1,725 students in Grades 7 through 12 and (see Tables 1 and 3 for percentages of student body and faculty/staff by race and/ or ethnicity and Table 2 for percentage of students enrolled in special programs). According to Federal poverty level income guidelines, 68% of the students qualify for free or reduced lunch.

The staff of Lincoln includes 82 faculty and staff members. There are 65 educators including teachers, administrators, and counselors. The administrative team consists of the principal, assistant principal, three guidance counselors, and a dean of students for each grade level. There are 55 teachers providing traditional instruction for Lincoln: 35% of them have been placed on action plans to improve their performance over the past 3 years. See Table 3 for a breakdown of educators by race/ethnicity.

There are 17 support staff members, including secretarial, custodial, and instructional support. See Table 4 for percentage of classified staff by race/ethnicity.

The students, like the majority of youth today, identify with the latest music genre, more specifically Hip Hop, the latest fashions, more specifically Hip Hop gear, and the latest form of communication including Apple iPods and Smartphones, Facebook, and tweeting.

Table 1. Percentage of student body by race/ethnicity

White	25%
African American	23%
Hispanic	20%
Lebanese	15%
Palestinian	13%
Native American, Asian, and Multiracial	4%

Table 2. Percentage of student body enrolled in special programs

Limited English Proficiency	32%
Academically gifted	12%
Title I remedial reading	55%
Exceptional children (special education)	15%

Table 3. Percentage of educators by race/ethnicity

White	80%
African American	10%
Hispanic	6%
Other (Asian, American Indian)	4%

Table 4. Percentage of classified staff by race/ethnicity

White	75%
African American	20%
Hispanic	5%

Testing data. When it comes to academics, Lincoln has not met adequate yearly progress (AYP) under the Federal No Child Left Behind (NCLB) Act for the past 2 years and, according to data from the State Department of Education (SDE), Lincoln did not reach 85% mastery as set by the state in the core academic areas: reading, math, science, civics, and writing. See Table 5 for testing data per grade level in the core areas.

Lincoln has become "the problem school" or "the ghetto" according to members of the community. At the last school board meeting, parents voiced their concerns regarding rumors that Lincoln was going to be closed at the end of the academic year

Table 5. Testing data per grade level in core areas

Grade	Reading (%)	Math (%)	Science (%)	Civics (%)	Writing (%)
Grade 7	30	43	21	29	11
Grade 8	47	59	33	42	27
Grade 9	20	31	44	15	29
Grade 10	67	51	78	81	49
Grade 11	52	45	61	58	72
Grade 12	73	68	55	83	46

because students had not met the state testing requirements in reading, math, science, civics, or writing. Many parents want to know who will replace Dr. Jones as the principal of Lincoln.

It has been rumored that Lincoln is in its current academic situation because the former superintendent and board members could not agree on instructional resources and many of the board members lobbied to fully support the early college program at Lincolnville Community and Technical College. The Hispanic community has begun a campaign to express their support for Mr. Azul. They believe he has the ability to unify the various fragmented student and parent communities of Lincoln; Dr. Jones concurs.

Cultural Wars

Currently, there are two Hispanic and two African American gangs located in Lincolnville, and Mr. Azul has served as a mediator and gang liaison for those students at Lincoln who are members of the Latin gangs. Dr. Jones is aware of this and applauds the efforts of Mr. Azul. Dr. Jones has asked a group of African American pastors of the local churches to work with the two African American gangs, but very little has come about. The Black churches in Lincolnville have been very supportive in mentoring Lincoln students over the years but are at a loss for how to deal with the gangs. Also, with the present global conflict in the Middle East, the Lebanese and Palestinian students are fighting at least 3 times a week. The students continue to say "the Zionists" are violating their civil rights. They are not allowed to pray during the day and feel that this is an attack on Islam and their religious beliefs. Dr. Jones, because of her commitment to the rights of students and the first amendment, on several occasions provided a classroom that points toward Mecca to allow the students to pray; however, many faculty members complain that this disrupts the instructional day.

Student Social Networking & Internet Sites

Megan Hudson, a senior and star forward on the girls' soccer team, happens to have one of the most popular social networking Internet sites at Lincoln. A cloudy video appeared on Megan's homepage via YouTube that has the entire town of

Lincolnville talking. The video is not clear, however—it appears to be Mr. Azul with Scott Jones, Dr. Jones's son, who happens to be a civil rights attorney and also the attorney for LISD. It is speculated the video clip is from a Gay, Lesbian, Bi-Sexual, and Transgendered (GLBT) Pride parade held in Washington, D.C. Many of the students do not believe it is "Coach TJ" on the video. Neither Dr. Jones nor Mr. Azul has made any comments. The parents of the students of Lincoln are divided along racial and ethnic lines regarding the video. Some are calling for Mr. Azul's resignation, whereas some others are calling for him to be named the principal of Lincoln. The local media has shown the video on the evening news and justified doing so by claiming the rights to the video were sold to them by Mr. and Mrs. Taylor Hudson, the parents of Megan Hudson, who currently serve as the co-presidents of the Lincoln PTSA. It is rumored that the video clip was sold for $10,000.

TEACHING NOTES

Lincoln Conversation: Issues for Reflection and Application

This case takes a fresh look at equity, leadership, accountability, and social justice in an age when the democratic promise of public education is at risk of being abandoned, forgotten, and emptied of meaning (Carlson & Gause, 2007). It navigates the multiple socio-cultural and political issues a superintendent, community member, educational leader, teacher, or principal might experience regarding demographic and cultural change. It is designed to assist students in developing the knowledge, skills, and dispositions to navigate micro-political environments that exist in learning communities. It is multi-layered and can be used in a variety of courses.

The United States is now more racially, culturally, and linguistically diverse than ever. Urbanization and immigration are key contributors to population growth and shifts, and the Southeast is a significant part of this change. North Carolina has the fastest growing Latino population in the nation (Johnson, 2002; Kitchen, 2004), as well as growing amounts of Asians and African Americans. In recent years, many school districts across the southeastern part of the United States have experienced a surge of students who have limited English skills. Educators are scrambling to determine how to serve different types of students and families given demographic shifts, while many families are in new places trying to adjust to unfamiliar school systems. Educational researchers are increasingly acknowledging the need to improve the practice of school leaders to meet the needs of underserved student communities. Teacher education and educational leadership preparation programs across the United States are experiencing a realignment of their curricula; however, what we teach is still insufficient to adequately prepare teachers and educational leaders to work in politically complex and multicultural learning environments (Lopez, 2003; Parker & Shapiro, 1992; Young & Laible, 2000).

Carlson and Gause (2007) assert

In its most radical terms this promise has been that public education can provide the basis for an informed, engaged citizenry, fully capable of their own self-governance, and armed with forms of critical consciousness that allow them to question the commonsense beliefs embedded in political speech and popular culture texts. Beyond this, the democratic promise of public education has been about "levelling the playing field" so that people are not held back, disadvantaged, or discriminated against by class, gender, race, sexual orientation, or other markers of difference and identity. This requires that public education be at the forefront in fighting entrenched systems of domination and oppression, and the institutional structures and commonsense beliefs that support them. (p. ix)

To teach, learn, and lead democratically requires the individual to engage in problem posing and critiquing taken-for-granted narratives of power and privilege. Critical change occurs with significant self-sacrifice, potential alienation/rejection, and costly consequences. As educators, we must do justice to the larger social/public responsibility of our positions, and we must exercise courage in making educational changes for social justice.

Reflective Case Questions

Vision Development
1. How are positional authority and democratic leadership represented?
2. As superintendent, how would you implement the district's vision?
3. As superintendent, how would you communicate a vision of learning for all students within the district and community?
4. If you were the superintendent, how would you negotiate the various subcultures present in your school district?

Instructional Leadership: Advocacy/Agency
1. How are the values of equity and social justice, democracy, caring, and meaningful learning reflected (or denied) in the culture of Lincoln?
2. What measures could the superintendent use to assess the culture and climate of the schools and/or district?
3. What initiatives would you implement at Lincoln High School to address the needs of the faculty and students regarding academic success?

Community Relations
1. What are the responsibilities of the superintendent/principal in collaborating with families and community members in the development of a meaningful learning community?
2. If you were the superintendent/principal, what course of action would you take to respond to the diverse community of the school/district?
3. How might you capitalize on the diversity of the school community to improve school programs and the needs of the students?
4. What role does the parent community play in the development of a successful school environment?

Cultural Context: Micro-political Dimensions of Leadership

1. How are the values of equity, democracy, and social justice reflected in Lincoln school district and/or Lincoln?
2. What social and cultural forces are at work within the city of Lincolnville, and how do these forces impact Lincoln Junior–Senior High?
3. Given the tenets of the socio-cultural implications of No Child Left Behind and state regulations, how might the intersections of race, class, and gender "inform" the leadership practice of the superintendent, principal, and assistant principal?
4. As superintendent, would you hire T. Jorge Azul as the new principal of Lincoln?

MINI CASE STUDY 1

Case Scenario

Alejandro Vasquez has just enrolled in Mango Elementary. His parents have informed you that he did well in his previous school. They have no official records, only his birth certificate and a report card from last year. According to the birth certificate, Alejandro is 8 years old; however, his physical appearance leads the staff to believe that he may be 11 years old. He appears to be very pleasant and speaks English well. As the principal of Mango, you have to make some decisions regarding the placement of Alejandro.

After placing Alejandro in Ms. Vance's 3rd grade class, you receive documentation that Alejandro has an IEP (Individualized Educational Plan) and that he has been retained twice.

What is your course of action?

Why did you choose this course of action?

How will this course of action impact Alejandro?

How will this course of action impact the school?

How will this course of action impact the teacher/classroom?

MINI CASE STUDY 2

Case Scenario

Walter Jones has just enrolled in Liberty Junior High School. His parents have informed you that he did well in his previous school. They have no official records, only his birth certificate and a report card from last year. According to the birth certificate, Walter is 12 years old; however, his physical appearance leads the staff to believe that he may be 14 years old. He appears to be very pleasant and speaks English well. You place Walter in the 7th grade and his homeroom teacher will be Ms. Smith.

After a week in school, Ms. Smith arrives at your door ranting and raving about Walter and how she wants him moved out of her homeroom. She cites several reasons that could be interpreted as racist and sexist. You talk with the other teachers regarding Walter and the only complaint has been that he is soft-spoken and likes to wear black fingernail polish and black lipstick, but the girls love him and the guys bully him sometimes.

What is your course of action?

Why did you choose this course of action?

How will this course of action impact Walter?

How will this course of action impact the school?

How will this course of action impact the teacher/classroom?

MINI CASE STUDY 3

Case Scenario

Victor Castillo has just enrolled in Grant Senior High School. His parents have informed you that he did well in his previous school. They have no official records, only his birth certificate and a report card from last year. According to the birth certificate, Victor is 16 years old; however, his physical appearance leads the staff to believe that he may be 19 years old. He appears to be very pleasant and speaks English well. You place Victor in the 11th grade and his homeroom teacher will be Mr. Johnson, who happens to be the school's soccer coach. His parents did indicate that Victor played soccer at his last school and was a part of the soccer team that won the state championship.

After three weeks of school, Mr. Johnson arrives at your door ranting and raving about Victor and how he is really doing a number on the soccer field. Mr. Johnson thinks that he has a champion soccer player on his team, but Victor's style of dress is controversial. You talk with the other teachers regarding Victor and the only complaint has been that he is soft-spoken and likes to wear black fingernail polish and black lipstick and that he wears headbands and "gang-like" clothing. The teachers also tell you that there is a rumor going around that Victor is supplying kids with prescription drugs and that he happens to be dating both Mr. and Miss Grant Senior High.

What is your course of action?

Why did you choose this course of action?

How will this course of action impact Victor?

How will this course of action impact the school?

How will this course of action impact the teacher/classroom?

INSTRUCTIONAL BEST PRACTICES FOR TEACHERS

Strategies and Techniques for Teaching Reading (Literature)

Teachers should do more of the following:

Read aloud to students daily

Schedule time for independent and group reading

Encourage students to choose their own reading materials

Expose students to multiple types of genres of literature

Encourage students to read fiction, non-fiction, science fiction, and mystery books

Model and discuss their own reading practices

Place emphasis on comprehension, context, and genre

Teach reading as a process

Use strategies that activate prior knowledge

Help students make and test predictions

Structure help during reading

Provide after-reading applications

Encourage social and collaborative activities with much discussion and group by interest and book choice

Silent reading should be followed by in-depth discussions

Teach literacy skills within the context of whole and meaningful literature

The writing process and writing activities should occur before and after reading activities

Use content specific text by discipline (e.g., historical novels in social studies)

Evaluate student progress by focusing on higher-order thinking skills

Teachers should do less of the following:

Emphasizing whole-class reading-group activities

Selecting all reading materials for individual/groups

Relying on basal readers

Keeping own reading habits private

Emphasizing reading sub-skills (word analysis, syllabication, and phonics)

Teaching the reading process as a single, one-step act

Assigning individual seat/desk work

Establishing reading groups by reading ability/level

Assigning round-robin oral reading

Teaching skills in phonics workbooks/drills in isolation

Limiting time to engage in the writing process

Discouraging pre-conventional spelling

Maintaining an established reading time

Focusing on individual low-level sub-skills

Measuring student reading success by a test score

Strategies for Teaching Writing

Teachers should do more of the following:

Student responsibility and ownership:
Allow students to choose their topics and measures for improvement
Conduct brief teacher-student conferences
Teach students how to review and monitor their progress

Class time spent on developing original work through:
Establishing real purposes for writing based on students' lived experiences
Encouraging students to become involved in the writing process

Providing instruction for all stages of the writing process
Utilizing the prewriting, drafting, revising, editing cycle
Modelling for students—drafting, revising, editing, and sharing—as a fellow author
Teaching grammar and mechanics in context, specifically at the editing stage, and as needed
Teaching students that writing is for real audiences and personal pleasure
Publishing works for the class, school, and greater community

Establish an affirming and supportive classroom setting for shared learning:
Actively exchange students' ideas
Value students' language and work
Promote small and large-group collaboration
Establish and encourage the peer critiquing and review process for improvement
Utilize writing across the curriculum as a tool for learning

Constructive and efficient evaluation that involves:
Providing informal and brief responses while students work
Evaluating and assessment a few student generated polished pieces
Focusing only on a few errors at a time
Looking for overall growth in students' self-evaluation
Encouraging open honest expression and risk taking

Teachers should do less of the following:

Control decision making by:
Deciding all writing topics
Dictating suggestions for improvement
Determining all learning objectives
Delivering whole-group instruction only

Spend a significant amount of instructional time on isolated drills on "sub-skills" (grammar, vocabulary, spelling, paragraphing, penmanship etc.)

Briefly give writing assignments without context or purpose, all in one step

Talk about the writing process without modelling or sharing

Deliver isolated grammar lessons in order based on textbook

Signal the teacher is the only one who reads assignments and/or student work

Devaluation of students' ideas by:
Viewing students as individuals with limited knowledge and language abilities
Treating students as a group of competing individuals
Focusing too much on students who are viewed as cheating, disruptive
Teaching writing only during "language arts" period, infrequently, and/or not at all.

Evaluation as negative burden for teacher and student by:
Grading papers heavily for errors only
Editing papers instead of allowing the student make improvements
Grading is punitive, primary focus on errors and not growth

Strategies for Teaching Mathematics

Teachers should do more of the following:

Connecting mathematics instruction to real-life "lived experiences"

Using manipulative activities as much as possible

Encouraging students to engage in cooperative/collaborative groups

Discussing mathematics and bring in real-life applications daily

Encouraging students to engage in questioning

Teaching students how to provide rationales and justifications for answers

Writing about mathematics

Focusing instruction on problem-solving

Recognizing content integration is key

Using computers, graphing calculators, and iPhone applications.

Facilitating the learning process

Evaluating and assessing learning as an integral part of instruction

Teaching mathematics as a major tool of real-life problem-solving

Providing multiple word problems with a variety of structures and solutions

Engaging students in everyday real world problems and applications

Incorporating multiple problem-solving strategies in lessons

Providing open-ended problems

Providing extended problem-solving projects as a form of instruction

Formulating and investigating questions from real-life problem situations

Teaching mathematics as a form of communication and language

Discussing mathematics

Reading mathematics

Engaging students in lessons on inductive and deductive reasoning

Teachers should do less of the following:

Utilizing the mathematics textbook at the expense of real-life problem-solving

Assigning lessons which rely on rote practice

Assigning lessons requiring students to engage in rote memorization of rules and formulas

Encouraging students to seek single answers and single methods to find answers

Devoting a significant amount of instructional time and learning activities dedicated to the use of drill worksheets

Devoting a significant amount of time dedicated to repetitive written exercises and practice

Teaching by telling and not by modelling

Teaching computation out of context

Stressing memorization excessively

Giving students mathematics tests for grades only and not to see students' growth

Establishing and maintaining a classroom where the teacher is viewed as the dispenser of knowledge

Discounting the importance of mathematics integration with other subjects and/or disciplines

Utilizing cue words for operation exercises

Requiring significant practice on routine and one-step problems

Requiring significant practice on problems by type

Communicating verbally and non-verbally that mathematics as a difficult subject and only few students will ever master the subject

Relying heavily on fill-in-the-blank worksheets

Allowing students to answer problems with yes or no responses

Allowing students to answer questions that need only numerical responses

Encouraging students to identify complex problems in simple terms

Relying on the teacher and/or answer key

Strategies for Teaching Science

Teachers should do more of the following:

Hands-on activities that include:
Students identifying their own questions involving the natural world
Observation learning activities designed by students
Instructional activities that focus on discovery and inquiry
Activities that encourage students to hypothesize to explain data
Instruction that allows students to engage the investigation process prior to information being presented
Activities in which students engage in self reflection throughout the instructional learning and activity process to realize concepts learned
Instructional activities which provide application to social issues, environmental concerns, and/or further scientific inquiry
Large and small group instruction should focus on underlying concepts about our natural world and how phenomena are explained.

Questioning, thinking, and problem solving, especially:
Encouraging students to question common and/or long-held beliefs
Establishing a willingness to embrace ambiguity when data aren't decisive
Creating a classroom/laboratory environment which encourages students to be open to changing their opinion
Using logic, planning inquiry-based activities, hypothesizing, inferring
Utilizing technology in instructional delivery and activities as much as possible
Facilitating in-depth study of important thematic topics
Creating a classroom culture of curiosity regarding nature and positive attitudes toward science for all students, including females and members of minority groups
Integrating reading, writing, and math in science instruction and units
Establishing collaborative small working groups with a focus on learning for all group members

Evaluation and assessment should focus on scientific concepts, processes, and attitudes.

Teachers should do less of the following:

Delivering science instruction based mainly on lecture and information giving

Depending on textbooks and simplistic patterns of instruction

Designing lab experiences where students follow steps without developing and answering their own questions

Treating students as if they have no knowledge or investigative abilities

Focusing on rote memorization of vocabulary, definitions, and explanations without connection to broader ideas

Encouraging students to work independently and competitively

Correcting students' perceptions of direct instruction

Isolating science from students' everyday lives and lived experiences

Providing superficial coverage of material based on scope-and-sequence

Believing only a few brilliant "nerds" can enjoy or succeed in science study

Adopting instructional activities limited to texts, lectures, and multiple-choice quizzes

Encouraging students to view Teacher as expert in subject matter versus students being seen as experts as well

Using evaluation and assessment focusing on memorization of detail and ignoring thinking skills, process skills, and attitudes

Strategies for Teaching Social Studies

Teachers should do more of the following:

Create a classroom that encourages students of all ability levels to engage in inter-active and cooperative learning

Provide instructional activities that encourage students to make choices about what to study

Create an environment where students discover the complexities of human interaction

Integrate social studies with other areas of the curriculum (e.g., language arts, science, mathematics)

Provide instruction in which students engage in inquiry and problem solving related to significant human issues

Create a classroom culture in which students make decisions and participate in wider social, political, and economic affairs; doing so will encourage students to develop a sense of shared responsibility for the welfare of their school and community

Provide richer and deeper levels of content in all grade levels, building on the prior knowledge children bring to social studies topics; this includes study of concepts from psychology, sociology, economics, and political science, as well as history and geography; students of all ages can understand, within their experience, American social institutions, issues for social groups, and problems of everyday living

Provide instruction through which students value and experience a "sense" of connected with humanity across American and global history, realizing the history and culture of diverse social groups, and the environment are all apart of social and historical systems

Encourage students to engage in inquiry with regard to their own cultural groups and communities to promote a sense of ownership

Evaluation and assessment should involve further learning and the promotion of responsible citizenship and open expression of concepts/ideas

Teachers should do less of the following:

Providing superficial coverage of curriculum based on scope and sequence, which covers everything but allows no time for a deeper understanding of topics

Requiring rote memorization of isolated facts in textbooks

Adopting instruction that isolates students from the actual exercise of responsible citizenship

Placing significant emphasis on reading about citizenship or future participation in the larger social and political world

Relying heavily on a lecture-style of instructional delivery

Assigning instructional activities that include only textbook reading and test taking

Devaluing student interest in social studies

Leaving out significant curriculum until secondary grades

Engaging in instructional practices that privilege one dominant cultural heritage and/or viewing having another cultural heritage as a deficit

Adopting instructional activities that leave students disconnected and unexcited about social studies

Using evaluation and assessment only at the end of a unit or grading period; using assessments that test only factual knowledge or memorization of textbook information

Strategies for Teaching the Related Arts (Visual Arts, Music, Dance, Physical Education, Theatre, Careers & Technology)

Teachers should do more of the following:

Related arts instruction should focus on doing, learning, and thinking

Instruction should focus on the process of creation, and not on the product

Instruction should highlight the steps and stages of careful craftsmanship

Focus more on student originality, their choice and responsibility in art making

Related arts should be viewed as an element of talent development for all students and not a select few who you may perceive as being "talented"

Class instruction should focus on the array of art forms, from Western and non-Western sources, different time periods, cultures, and ethnic groups

Develop and support every student's quest to discover his or her personal media, style, and tastes

The arts should be a viable part of the school day and curriculum

Integrate related arts across the curriculum

Provide reasonable class loads and work assignments for related arts-specialist teachers; they should not be viewed as "baby-sitters," or proctors for tests

School and classroom instruction should be facilitated by artists in schools, both as performers and as partners with art teachers

Establish and maintain long-term partnerships with artists and arts organizations

Every member of the school community and the greater community at large should be involved with the arts

Teachers should do less of the following:

Emphasizing the studying of other people's artworks

Providing art instruction and/or projects requiring students to create identical products

Placing extreme focus on final products and not celebrating learning process

Encouraging students to view art (Related Arts) as an arena for competition, screening, awards, and prizes

Promoting an exclusive focus on Western, high-culture, elite art forms disconnected from a wide range of art making/production

Allowing students to explore too many art forms and not encourage mastery

Relegating arts only to the Related Arts teachers, not provided by the classroom teacher

Providing arts classes that lack intensity and that occur only once a week.

Overloading Related Arts teachers with multiple classes

Allowing Physical Education to be viewed as only athletics

Utilizing instructional time for skill development and not expression

Believing only certain types of students can participate in the arts program

Stereotyping and/or typecasting students based upon race, class, and gender

Using evaluation and assessment of student progress based upon final products and not growth

WEBSITES

ABD Not Me!
www.abdnotme.com
This site is for all of those individuals who are currently completing terminal degrees, those who have completed course-work but nothing else, those who are having difficulty beginning and/or completing the dissertation process, and those who are feeling lost within the process. After witnessing many of my dissertators have "emotional" and "mental" breakdowns all within the same week and listening to each of them make the following statements: "I must be stupid," "I know I am the

only one going through this," and "I feel so alone and disconnected," I realized an online support community would be great for them and others.

American Civil Liberties Union
www.aclu.org

Anti-Defamation League
www.adl.org

Association for the Study of African American Life and History
www.asalh.org

Black Male PhD
www.blackmalephd.com
Forum, resources, links, and support for "Brothers" with terminal degrees and for those who aspire to achieve their terminal degree

Black Masculinity
www.blackmasculinity.com
A site designed to critique, question, and de-center Black Masculinity

Center for Multicultural Education at The University of Washington
http://education.washington.edu/cme/view.htm

Center for the Study of Race, Culture, and Politics at The University of Chicago
http://csrpc.uchicago.edu

Center on Education Policy
www.cep-dc.org

Facing History and Ourselves
www.facinghistory.org

Gay and Lesbian Alliance Against Defamation
www.glaad.org

GLBTIQQ
www.glbtiqq.com
Forum, resources, educational materials, and support for those who self-identify within the following continuum: Gay, Lesbian, Bi-sexual, Transgendered, Intersex, Queer, and Questioning. This site is also designed for allies, educators, those individuals who love GLBTIQQ peoples, as well as a place to investigate, interrogate, and question the heteronormative.

Gay, Lesbian, and Straight Education Network
www.glsen.org

Human Rights Campaign
www.hrc.org

National Association for Diversity Officers in Higher Education
www.nadohe.org

National Association for Multicultural Education
www.nameorg.org

NAACP–National Association for the Advancement of Colored People
www.naacp.org

National Center for Lesbian Rights
www.nclrights.org

National Council of La Raza
www.nclr.org

National Gay and Lesbian Task Force
www.thetaskforce.org

National Urban League
www.nul.org

Parents, Families, & Friends of Lesbians and Gays
www.pflag.org

Southern Poverty Law Center
www.splcenter.org

Teaching Tolerance
www.tolerance.org

The Center for Diversity Education
www.diversityed.org

The Freire Project
http://www.freireproject.org

The International Civil Rights Center & Museum
www.sitinmovement.org

The National Conference for Community and Justice-Piedmont Triad
www.nccjtriad.org

The Principal's Desk
www.theprincipalsdesk.com
Forum, resources, and links for practicing & aspiring principals

The Superintendent's Desk
www.thesuperintendentsdesk.com
Forum, resources, and links for practicing & aspiring superintendents

The Vice-Principal's Desk
www.theviceprincipalsdesk.com
Forum, resources, and links for practicing & aspiring vice principals

UNCG-OEDI
www.uncgoedi.com
This site serves as a forum, provides resources, links and ideas for the UNC, Greensboro Office of Equity, Diversity, and Inclusion. This site is not an official site of UNCG and it is not sanctioned by UNC, Greensboro.

Urban Institute
www.urban.org

Understanding Race
www.understandingrace.org

United States Commission on Civil Rights
www.usccr.gov

United States Department of Education
www.ed.gov

PRESIDENT LYNDON BAINES JOHNSON: COMMENCEMENT ADDRESS AT HOWARD UNIVERSITY

On June 4, 1965, U.S. President Lyndon Baines Johnson gave the commencement address at Howard University in Washington, D.C. He used the occasion to remind his audience and the nation of the long history of racial discrimination and urged the American people to end racial discrimination as the most important step in ensuring equality among all of its citizens.

Dr. Nabrit, my fellow Americans:

I am delighted at the chance to speak at this important and this historic institution. Howard has long been an outstanding center for the education of Negro Americans. Its students are of every race and color and they come from many countries of the world. It is truly a working example of democratic excellence.

Our earth is the home of revolution. In every corner of every continent men charged with hope contend with ancient ways in the pursuit of justice. They reach for the newest of weapons to realize the oldest of dreams, that each may walk in freedom and pride, stretching his talents, enjoying the fruits of the earth.

Our enemies may occasionally seize the day of change, but it is the banner of our revolution they take. And our own future is linked to this process of swift and turbulent change in many lands in the world. But nothing in any country touches us more profoundly, and nothing is more freighted with meaning for our own destiny than the revolution of the Negro American.

In far too many ways American Negroes have been another nation: deprived of freedom, crippled by hatred, the doors of opportunity closed to hope.

In our time change has come to this Nation, too. The American Negro, acting with impressive restraint, has peacefully protested and marched, entered the courtrooms and the seats of government, demanding a justice that has long been denied. The voice of the Negro was the call to action. But it is a tribute to America that, once aroused, the courts and the Congress, the President and most of the people, have been the allies of progress.

LEGAL PROTECTION FOR HUMAN RIGHTS

Thus we have seen the high court of the country declare that discrimination based on race was repugnant to the Constitution, and therefore void. We have seen in 1957, and 1960, and again in 1964, the first civil rights legislation in this Nation in almost an entire century.

As majority leader of the United States Senate, I helped to guide two of these bills through the Senate. And, as your President, I was proud to sign the third. And now very soon we will have the fourth–a new law guaranteeing every American the right to vote.

No act of my entire administration will give me greater satisfaction than the day when my signature makes this bill, too, the law of this land.

The voting rights bill will be the latest, and among the most important, in a long series of victories. But this victory–as Winston Churchill said of another triumph for freedom– "is not the end. It is not even the beginning of the end. But it is, perhaps, the end of the beginning."

That beginning is freedom; and the barriers to that freedom are tumbling down. Freedom is the right to share, share fully and equally, in American society–to vote, to hold a job, to enter a public place, to go to school. It is the right to be treated in every part of our national life as a person equal in dignity and promise to all others.

FREEDOM IS NOT ENOUGH

But freedom is not enough. You do not wipe away the scars of centuries by saying: Now you are free to go where you want, and do as you desire, and choose the leaders you please.

You do not take a person who, for years, has been hobbled by chains and liberate him, bring him up to the starting line of a race and then say, "you are free to compete with all the others," and still justly believe that you have been completely fair.

Thus it is not enough just to open the gates of opportunity. All our citizens must have the ability to walk through those gates.

This is the next and the more profound stage of the battle for civil rights. We seek not just freedom but opportunity. We seek not just legal equity but human ability, not just equality as a right and a theory but equality as a fact and equality as a result.

For the task is to give 20 million Negroes the same chance as every other American to learn and grow, to work and share in society, to develop their abilities–physical, mental and spiritual, and to pursue their individual happiness.

To this end equal opportunity is essential, but not enough, not enough. Men and women of all races are born with the same range of abilities. But ability is not just the product of birth. Ability is stretched or stunted by the family that you live with, and the neighborhood you live in–by the school you go to and the poverty or the richness of your surroundings. It is the product of a hundred unseen forces playing upon the little infant, the child, and finally the man.

PROGRESS FOR SOME

This graduating class at Howard University is witness to the indomitable determination of the Negro American to win his way in American life.

The number of Negroes in schools of higher learning has almost doubled in 15 years. The number of non-White professional workers has more than doubled in 10 years.

The median income of Negro college women tonight exceeds that of White college women. And there are also the enormous accomplishments of distinguished individual Negroes–many of them graduates of this institution, and one of them the first lady ambassador in the history of the United States.

These are proud and impressive achievements. But they tell only the story of a growing middle class minority, steadily narrowing the gap between them and their White counterparts.

A WIDENING GULF

But for the great majority of Negro Americans-the poor, the unemployed, the uprooted, and the dispossessed–there is a much grimmer story. They still, as we meet here tonight, are another nation. Despite the court orders and the laws, despite the legislative victories and the speeches, for them the walls are rising and the gulf is widening.

Here are some of the facts of this American failure.

Thirty-five years ago the rate of unemployment for Negroes and Whites was about the same. Tonight the Negro rate is twice as high.

In 1948 the 8 percent unemployment rate for Negro teenage boys was actually less than that of Whites. By last year that rate had grown to 23 percent, as against 13 percent for Whites unemployed.

Between 1949 and 1959, the income of Negro men relative to White men declined in every section of this country. From 1952 to 1963 the median income of Negro families compared to White actually dropped from 57 percent to 53 percent.

In the years 1955 through 1957, 22 percent of experienced Negro workers were out of work at some time during the year. In 1961 through 1963 that proportion had soared to 29 percent.

Since 1947 the number of White families living in poverty has decreased 27 percent while the number of poorer non-White families decreased only 3 percent.

The infant mortality of non-Whites in 1940 was 70 percent greater than Whites. Twenty-two years later it was 90 percent greater.

Moreover, the isolation of Negro from White communities is increasing, rather than decreasing as Negroes crowd into the central cities and become a city within a city.

Of course Negro Americans as well as White Americans have shared in our rising national abundance. But the harsh fact of the matter is that in the battle for true equality too many–far too many–are losing ground every day.

THE CAUSES OF INEQUALITY

We are not completely sure why this is. We know the causes are complex and subtle. But we do know the two broad basic reasons. And we do know that we have to act.

First, Negroes are trapped–as many Whites are trapped–in inherited, gateless poverty. They lack training and skills. They are shut in, in slums, without decent medical care. Private and public poverty combine to cripple their capacities.

We are trying to attack these evils through our poverty program, through our education program, through our medical care and our other health programs, and a dozen more of the Great Society programs that are aimed at the root causes of this poverty.

We will increase, and we will accelerate, and we will broaden this attack in years to come until this most enduring of foes finally yields to our unyielding will.

But there is a second cause–much more difficult to explain, more deeply grounded, more desperate in its force. It is the devastating heritage of long years of slavery; and a century of oppression, hatred, and injustice.

SPECIAL NATURE OF NEGRO POVERTY

For Negro poverty is not White poverty. Many of its causes and many of its cures are the same. But there are differences-deep, corrosive, obstinate differences–radiating painful roots into the community, and into the family, and the nature of the individual.

These differences are not racial differences. They are solely and simply the consequence of ancient brutality, past injustice, and present prejudice. They are anguishing to observe. For the Negro they are a constant reminder of oppression. For the White they are a constant reminder of guilt. But they must be faced and they must be dealt with and they must be overcome, if we are ever to reach the time when the only difference between Negroes and Whites is the color of their skin.

Nor can we find a complete answer in the experience of other American minorities. They made a valiant and a largely successful effort to emerge from poverty and prejudice.

The Negro, like these others, will have to rely mostly upon his own efforts. But he just can not do it alone. For they did not have the heritage of centuries to overcome, and they did not have a cultural tradition which had been twisted and battered by endless years of hatred and hopelessness, nor were they excluded–these others–because of race or color–a feeling whose dark intensity is matched by no other prejudice in our society.

Nor can these differences be understood as isolated infirmities. They are a seamless web. They cause each other. They result from each other. They reinforce each other.

Much of the Negro community is buried under a blanket of history and circumstance. It is not a lasting solution to lift just one corner of that blanket. We must stand on all sides and we must raise the entire cover if we are to liberate our fellow citizens.

THE ROOTS OF INJUSTICE

One of the differences is the increased concentration of Negroes in our cities. More than 73 percent of all Negroes live in urban areas compared with less than 70 percent of the Whites. Most of these Negroes live in slums. Most of these Negroes live together–a separated people.

Men are shaped by their world. When it is a world of decay, ringed by an invisible wall, when escape is arduous and uncertain, and the saving pressures of a more hopeful society are unknown, it can cripple the youth and it can desolate the men.

There is also the burden that a dark skin can add to the search for a productive place in our society. Unemployment strikes most swiftly and broadly at the Negro, and this burden erodes hope. Blighted hope breeds despair.

Despair brings indifferences to the learning which offers a way out. And despair, coupled with indifferences, is often the source of destructive rebellion against the fabric of society.

There is also the lacerating hurt of early collision with White hatred or prejudice, distaste or condescension. Other groups have felt similar intolerance. But success and achievement could wipe it away. They do not change the color of a man's skin. I have seen this uncomprehending pain in the eyes of the little, young Mexican-American schoolchildren that I taught many years ago. But it can be overcome. But, for many, the wounds are always open.

FAMILY BREAKDOWN

Perhaps most important–its influence radiating to every part of life–is the breakdown of the Negro family structure. For this, most of all, White America must accept responsibility. It flows from centuries of oppression and persecution of the Negro man. It flows from the long years of degradation and discrimination, which have attacked his dignity and assaulted his ability to produce for his family.

This, too, is not pleasant to look upon. But it must be faced by those whose serious intent is to improve the life of all Americans.

Only a minority–less than half–of all Negro children reach the age of 18 having lived all their lives with both of their parents. At this moment, tonight, little less than two-thirds are at home with both of their parents. Probably a majority of all Negro children receive federally-aided public assistance sometime during their childhood.

The family is the cornerstone of our society. More than any other force it shapes the attitude, the hopes, the ambitions, and the values of the child. And when the family collapses it is the children that are usually damaged. When it happens on a massive scale the community itself is crippled.

So, unless we work to strengthen the family, to create conditions under which most parents will stay together–all the rest: schools, and playgrounds, and public assistance, and private concern, will never be enough to cut completely the circle of despair and deprivation.

TO FULFILL THESE RIGHTS

There is no single easy answer to all of these problems.

Jobs are part of the answer. They bring the income which permits a man to provide for his family.

Decent homes in decent surroundings and a chance to learn–an equal chance to learn–are part of the answer.

Welfare and social programs better designed to hold families together are part of the answer.

Care for the sick is part of the answer.

An understanding heart by all Americans is another big part of the answer.

And to all of these fronts–and a dozen more–I will dedicate the expanding efforts of the Johnson administration.

But there are other answers that are still to be found. Nor do we fully understand even all of the problems. Therefore, I want to announce tonight that this fall I intend to call a White House conference of scholars, and experts, and outstanding Negro leaders–men of both races–and officials of Government at every level.

This White House conference's theme and title will be "To Fulfill These Rights." Its object will be to help the American Negro fulfill the rights which, after the long time of injustice, he is finally about to secure.

To move beyond opportunity to achievement.

To shatter forever not only the barriers of law and public practice, but the walls which bound the condition of many by the color of his skin.

To dissolve, as best we can, the antique enmities of the heart which diminish the holder, divide the great democracy, and do wrong–great wrong–to the children of God.

And I pledge you tonight that this will be a chief goal of my administration, and of my program next year, and in the years to come. And I hope, and I pray, and I believe, it will be a part of the program of all America.

WHAT IS JUSTICE

For what is justice?

It is to fulfill the fair expectations of man.

Thus, American justice is a very special thing. For, from the first, this has been a land of towering expectations. It was to be a nation where each man could be ruled by the common consent of all–enshrined in law, given life by institutions, guided by men themselves subject to its rule. And all–all of every station and origin–would be touched equally in obligation and in liberty.

Beyond the law lay the land. It was a rich land, glowing with more abundant promise than man had ever seen. Here, unlike any place yet known, all were to share the harvest.

And beyond this was the dignity of man. Each could become whatever his qualities of mind and spirit would permit–to strive, to seek, and, if he could, to find his happiness.

This is American justice. We have pursued it faithfully to the edge of our imperfections, and we have failed to find it for the American Negro.

So, it is the glorious opportunity of this generation to end the one huge wrong of the American Nation and, in so doing, to find America for ourselves, with the same immense thrill of discovery which gripped those who first began to realize that here, at last, was a home for freedom.

All it will take is for all of us to understand what this country is and what this country must become.

The Scripture promises: "I shall light a candle of understanding in thine heart, which shall not be put out."

Together, and with millions more, we can light that candle of understanding in the heart of all America.

And, once lit, it will never again go out.

(Accessed and retrieved June 10, 2010 http://www.blackpast.org/?q=1965-president-lyndon-b-johnson-fulfill-these-rights)

Lyndon Baines Johnson Library and Museum-Accessed and retrieved June 10, 2010 http://www.lbjlib.utexas.edu/johnson/archives.hom/speeches.hom/650604.asp

THE DECLARATION OF INDEPENDENCE

IN CONGRESS, JULY 4, 1776

The unanimous Declaration of the thirteen united States of America

When in the Course of human events it becomes necessary for one people to dissolve the political bands which have connected them with another and to assume among the powers of the earth, the separate and equal station to which the Laws of Nature and of Nature's God entitle them, a decent respect to the opinions of mankind requires that they should declare the causes which impel them to the separation.

We hold these truths to be self-evident, that all men are created equal, that they are endowed by their Creator with certain unalienable Rights, that among these are Life, Liberty and the pursuit of Happiness. — That to secure these rights, Governments are instituted among Men, deriving their just powers from the consent of the governed, — That whenever any Form of Government becomes destructive of these ends, it is the Right of the People to alter or to abolish it, and to institute new Government, laying its foundation on such principles and organizing its powers in such form, as to them shall seem most likely to effect their Safety and Happiness. Prudence, indeed, will dictate that Governments long established should not be changed for light and transient causes; and accordingly all experience hath shewn that mankind are more disposed to suffer, while evils are sufferable than to right themselves by abolishing the forms to which they are accustomed. But when a long train of abuses and usurpations, pursuing invariably the same Object evinces a design to reduce them under absolute Despotism, it is their right, it is their duty, to throw off such Government, and to provide new Guards for their future security. — Such has been the patient sufferance of these Colonies; and such is now the necessity which constrains them to alter their former Systems of Government. The history of the present King of Great Britain is a history of repeated injuries and usurpations, all having in direct object the establishment of an absolute Tyranny over these States. To prove this, let Facts be submitted to a candid world.

He has refused his Assent to Laws, the most wholesome and necessary for the public good.

He has forbidden his Governors to pass Laws of immediate and pressing importance, unless suspended in their operation till his Assent should be obtained; and when so suspended, he has utterly neglected to attend to them.

He has refused to pass other Laws for the accommodation of large districts of people, unless those people would relinquish the right of Representation in the Legislature, a right inestimable to them and formidable to tyrants only.

He has called together legislative bodies at places unusual, uncomfortable, and distant from the depository of their Public Records, for the sole purpose of fatiguing them into compliance with his measures.

He has dissolved Representative Houses repeatedly, for opposing with manly firmness his invasions on the rights of the people.

He has refused for a long time, after such dissolutions, to cause others to be elected, whereby the Legislative Powers, incapable of Annihilation, have returned to the People at large for their exercise; the State remaining in the mean time exposed to all the dangers of invasion from without, and convulsions within.

He has endeavoured to prevent the population of these States; for that purpose obstructing the Laws for Naturalization of Foreigners; refusing to pass others to encourage their migrations hither, and raising the conditions of new Appro-priations of Lands.

He has obstructed the Administration of Justice by refusing his Assent to Laws for establishing Judiciary Powers.

He has made Judges dependent on his Will alone for the tenure of their offices, and the amount and payment of their salaries.

He has erected a multitude of New Offices, and sent hither swarms of Officers to harass our people and eat out their substance.

He has kept among us, in times of peace, Standing Armies without the Consent of our legislatures.

He has affected to render the Military independent of and superior to the Civil Power.

He has combined with others to subject us to a jurisdiction foreign to our constitution, and unacknowledged by our laws; giving his Assent to their Acts of pretended Legislation:

For quartering large bodies of armed troops among us:

For protecting them, by a mock Trial from punishment for any Murders which they should commit on the Inhabitants of these States:

For cutting off our Trade with all parts of the world:

For imposing Taxes on us without our Consent:

For depriving us in many cases, of the benefit of Trial by Jury:

For transporting us beyond Seas to be tried for pretended offences:

For abolishing the free System of English Laws in a neighbouring Province, establishing therein an Arbitrary government, and enlarging its Boundaries so as to render it at once an example and fit instrument for introducing the same absolute rule into these Colonies:

For taking away our Charters, abolishing our most valuable Laws and altering fundamentally the Forms of our Governments:

For suspending our own Legislatures, and declaring themselves invested with power to legislate for us in all cases whatsoever.

He has abdicated Government here, by declaring us out of his Protection and waging War against us.

He has plundered our seas, ravaged our coasts, burnt our towns, and destroyed the lives of our people.

He is at this time transporting large Armies of foreign Mercenaries to compleat the works of death, desolation, and tyranny, already begun with circumstances of Cruelty & Perfidy scarcely paralleled in the most barbarous ages, and totally unworthy the Head of a civilized nation.

He has constrained our fellow Citizens taken Captive on the high Seas to bear Arms against their Country, to become the executioners of their friends and Brethren, or to fall themselves by their Hands.

He has excited domestic insurrections amongst us, and has endeavoured to bring on the inhabitants of our frontiers, the merciless Indian Savages whose known rule of warfare is an undistinguished destruction of all ages, sexes and conditions.

In every stage of these Oppressions We have Petitioned for Redress in the most humble terms: Our repeated Petitions have been answered only by repeated injury. A Prince, whose character is thus marked by every act which may define a Tyrant, is unfit to be the ruler of a free people.

Nor have We been wanting in attentions to our British brethren. We have warned them from time to time of attempts by their legislature to extend an unwarrantable jurisdiction over us. We have reminded them of the circumstances of our emigration and settlement here. We have appealed to their native justice and magnanimity, and we have conjured them by the ties of our common kindred to disavow these usurpations, which would inevitably interrupt our connections and correspondence. They too have been deaf to the voice of justice and of consanguinity. We must, therefore, acquiesce in the necessity, which denounces our Separation, and hold them, as we hold the rest of mankind, Enemies in War, in Peace Friends.

We, therefore, the Representatives of the united States of America, in General Congress, Assembled, appealing to the Supreme Judge of the world for the rectitude of our intentions, do, in the Name, and by Authority of the good People of these Colonies, solemnly publish and declare, That these united Colonies are, and of Right ought to be Free and Independent States, that they are Absolved from all Allegiance to the British Crown, and that all political connection between them and the State of Great Britain, is and ought to be totally dissolved; and that as Free and Independent States, they have full Power to levy War, conclude Peace, contract Alliances, establish Commerce, and to do all other Acts and Things which Independent States may of right do. — And for the support of this Declaration, with a firm reliance on the protection of Divine Providence, we mutually pledge to each other our Lives, our Fortunes, and our sacred Honor.

— John Hancock

New Hampshire: Josiah Bartlett, William Whipple, Matthew Thornton

Massachusetts: John Hancock, Samuel Adams, John Adams, Robert Treat Paine, Elbridge Gerry

Rhode Island: Stephen Hopkins, William Ellery

Connecticut: Roger Sherman, Samuel Huntington, William Williams, Oliver Wolcott

New York: William Floyd, Philip Livingston, Francis Lewis, Lewis Morris

New Jersey: Richard Stockton, John Witherspoon, Francis Hopkinson, John Hart, Abraham Clark

Pennsylvania: Robert Morris, Benjamin Rush, Benjamin Franklin, John Morton, George Clymer, James Smith, George Taylor, James Wilson, George Ross

Delaware: Caesar Rodney, George Read, Thomas McKean

Maryland: Samuel Chase, William Paca, Thomas Stone, Charles Carroll of Carrollton

Virginia: George Wythe, Richard Henry Lee, Thomas Jefferson, Benjamin Harrison, Thomas Nelson, Jr., Francis Lightfoot Lee, Carter Braxton

North Carolina: William Hooper, Joseph Hewes, John Penn

South Carolina: Edward Rutledge, Thomas Heyward, Jr., Thomas Lynch, Jr., Arthur Middleton

Georgia: Button Gwinnett, Lyman Hall, George Walton

Accessed and Retrieved: June 11, 2010 http://www.ushistory.org/DECLA RATION/document/index.htm

THE CONSTITUTION OF THE UNITED STATES OF AMERICA

We the people of the United States, in order to form a more perfect union, establish justice, insure domestic tranquillity, provide for the common defense, promote the general welfare, and secure the blessings of liberty to ourselves and our posterity, do ordain and establish this Constitution for the United States of America.

Article I

Section 1. All legislative powers herein granted shall be vested in a Congress of the United States, which shall consist of a Senate and House of Representatives.

Section 2. The House of Representatives shall be composed of members chosen every second year by the people of the several states, and the electors in each state shall have the qualifications requisite for electors of the most numerous branch of the state legislature.

No person shall be a Representative who shall not have attained to the age of twenty five years, and been seven years a citizen of the United States, and who shall not, when elected, be an inhabitant of that state in which he shall be chosen.

Representatives and direct taxes shall be apportioned among the several states which may be included within this union, according to their respective numbers, which shall be determined by adding to the whole number of free persons, including those bound to service for a term of years, and excluding Indians not taxed, three fifths of all other Persons. The actual Enumeration shall be made within three years after the first meeting of the Congress of the United States, and within every subsequent term of ten years, in such manner as they shall by law direct. The number of Representatives shall not exceed one for every thirty thousand, but each state shall have at least one Representative; and until such enumeration shall be made, the state of New Hampshire shall be entitled to chuse three, Massachusetts eight, Rhode Island and Providence Plantations one, Connecticut five, New York six, New Jersey four, Pennsylvania eight, Delaware one, Maryland six, Virginia ten, North Carolina five, South Carolina five, and Georgia three.

When vacancies happen in the Representation from any state, the executive authority thereof shall issue writs of election to fill such vacancies.

The House of Representatives shall choose their speaker and other officers; and shall have the sole power of impeachment.

Section 3. The Senate of the United States shall be composed of two Senators from each state, chosen by the legislature thereof, for six years; and each Senator shall have one vote.

Immediately after they shall be assembled in consequence of the first election, they shall be divided as equally as may be into three classes. The seats of the Senators of the first class shall be vacated at the expiration of the second year, of the second class at the expiration of the fourth year, and the third class at the expiration of the sixth year, so that one third may be chosen every second year; and if vacancies happen by resignation, or otherwise, during the recess of the legislature of any state, the executive thereof may make temporary appointments until the next meeting of the legislature, which shall then fill such vacancies.

No person shall be a Senator who shall not have attained to the age of thirty years, and been nine years a citizen of the United States and who shall not, when elected, be an inhabitant of that state for which he shall be chosen.

The Vice President of the United States shall be President of the Senate, but shall have no vote, unless they be equally divided.

The Senate shall choose their other officers, and also a President pro tempore, in the absence of the Vice President, or when he shall exercise the office of President of the United States.

The Senate shall have the sole power to try all impeachments. When sitting for that purpose, they shall be on oath or affirmation. When the President of the United States is tried, the Chief Justice shall preside: And no person shall be convicted without the concurrence of two thirds of the members present.

Judgment in cases of impeachment shall not extend further than to removal from office, and disqualification to hold and enjoy any office of honor, trust or profit under the United States: but the party convicted shall nevertheless be liable and subject to indictment, trial, judgment and punishment, according to law.

Section 4. The times, places and manner of holding elections for Senators and Representatives, shall be prescribed in each state by the legislature thereof; but the Congress may at any time by law make or alter such regulations, except as to the places of choosing Senators.

The Congress shall assemble at least once in every year, and such meeting shall be on the first Monday in December, unless they shall by law appoint a different day.

Section 5. Each House shall be the judge of the elections, returns and qualifications of its own members, and a majority of each shall constitute a quorum to do business; but a smaller number may adjourn from day to day, and may be authorized to compel the attendance of absent members, in such manner, and under such penalties as each House may provide.

Each House may determine the rules of its proceedings, punish its members for disorderly behavior, and, with the concurrence of two thirds, expel a member.

Each House shall keep a journal of its proceedings, and from time to time publish the same, excepting such parts as may in their judgment require secrecy; and the yeas and nays of the members of either House on any question shall, at the desire of one fifth of those present, be entered on the journal.

Neither House, during the session of Congress, shall, without the consent of the other, adjourn for more than three days, nor to any other place than that in which the two Houses shall be sitting.

Section 6. The Senators and Representatives shall receive a compensation for their services, to be ascertained by law, and paid out of the treasury of the United States. They shall in all cases, except treason, felony and breach of the peace, be privileged from arrest during their attendance at the session of their respective Houses, and in going to and returning from the same; and for any speech or debate in either House, they shall not be questioned in any other place.

No Senator or Representative shall, during the time for which he was elected, be appointed to any civil office under the authority of the United States, which shall have been created, or the emoluments whereof shall have been increased during such time: and no person holding any office under the United States, shall be a member of either House during his continuance in office.

Section 7. All bills for raising revenue shall originate in the House of Representatives; but the Senate may propose or concur with amendments as on other Bills.

Every bill which shall have passed the House of Representatives and the Senate, shall, before it become a law, be presented to the President of the United States; if he approve he shall sign it, but if not he shall return it, with his objections to that House in which it shall have originated, who shall enter the objections at large on their journal, and proceed to reconsider it. If after such reconsideration two thirds of that House shall agree to pass the bill, it shall be sent, together with the objections, to the other House, by which it shall likewise be reconsidered, and if approved by two thirds of that House, it shall become a law. But in all such cases the votes of both Houses shall be determined by yeas and nays, and the names of the persons voting for and against the bill shall be entered on the journal of each House respectively. If any bill shall not be returned by the President within ten days (Sundays excepted) after it shall have been presented to him, the same shall be a law, in like manner as if he had signed it, unless the Congress by their adjournment prevent its return, in which case it shall not be a law.

Every order, resolution, or vote to which the concurrence of the Senate and House of Representatives may be necessary (except on a question of adjournment) shall be presented to the President of the United States; and before the same shall take effect, shall be approved by him, or being disapproved by him, shall be passed by two thirds of the Senate and House of Representatives, according to the rules and limitations prescribed in the case of a bill.

Section 8. The Congress shall have power to lay and collect taxes, duties, imposts and excises, to pay the debts and provide for the common defense and general welfare of the United States; but all duties, imposts and excises shall be uniform throughout the United States;

To borrow money on the credit of the United States;

To regulate commerce with foreign nations, and among the several states, and with the Indian tribes;

To establish a uniform rule of naturalization, and uniform laws on the subject of bankruptcies throughout the United States;

To coin money, regulate the value thereof, and of foreign coin, and fix the standard of weights and measures;

To provide for the punishment of counterfeiting the securities and current coin of the United States;

To establish post offices and post roads;

To promote the progress of science and useful arts, by securing for limited times to authors and inventors the exclusive right to their respective writings and discoveries;

To constitute tribunals inferior to the Supreme Court;

To define and punish piracies and felonies committed on the high seas, and offenses against the law of nations;

To declare war, grant letters of marque and reprisal, and make rules concerning captures on land and water;

To raise and support armies, but no appropriation of money to that use shall be for a longer term than two years;

To provide and maintain a navy;

To make rules for the government and regulation of the land and naval forces;

To provide for calling forth the militia to execute the laws of the union, suppress insurrections and repel invasions;

To provide for organizing, arming, and disciplining, the militia, and for governing such part of them as may be employed in the service of the United States, reserving to the states respectively, the appointment of the officers, and the authority of training the militia according to the discipline prescribed by Congress;

To exercise exclusive legislation in all cases whatsoever, over such District (not exceeding ten miles square) as may, by cession of particular states, and the acceptance of Congress, become the seat of the government of the United States, and to exercise like authority over all places purchased by the consent of the legislature of the state in which the same shall be, for the erection of forts, magazines, arsenals, dockyards, and other needful buildings;–And

To make all laws which shall be necessary and proper for carrying into execution the foregoing powers, and all other powers vested by this Constitution in the government of the United States, or in any department or officer thereof.

Section 9. The migration or importation of such persons as any of the states now existing shall think proper to admit, shall not be prohibited by the Congress prior to the year one thousand eight hundred and eight, but a tax or duty may be imposed on such importation, not exceeding ten dollars for each person.

The privilege of the writ of habeas corpus shall not be suspended, unless when in cases of rebellion or invasion the public safety may require it.

No bill of attainder or ex post facto Law shall be passed.

No capitation, or other direct, tax shall be laid, unless in proportion to the census or enumeration herein before directed to be taken.

No tax or duty shall be laid on articles exported from any state.

No preference shall be given by any regulation of commerce or revenue to the ports of one state over those of another: nor shall vessels bound to, or from, one state, be obliged to enter, clear or pay duties in another.

No money shall be drawn from the treasury, but in consequence of appropriations made by law; and a regular statement and account of receipts and expenditures of all public money shall be published from time to time.

No title of nobility shall be granted by the United States: and no person holding any office of profit or trust under them, shall, without the consent of the Congress, accept of any present, emolument, office, or title, of any kind whatever, from any king, prince, or foreign state.

Section 10. No state shall enter into any treaty, alliance, or confederation; grant letters of marque and reprisal; coin money; emit bills of credit; make anything but gold and silver coin a tender in payment of debts; pass any bill of attainder, ex post facto law, or law impairing the obligation of contracts, or grant any title of nobility.

No state shall, without the consent of the Congress, lay any imposts or duties on imports or exports, except what may be absolutely necessary for executing its inspection laws: and the net produce of all duties and imposts, laid by any state on imports or exports, shall be for the use of the treasury of the United States; and all such laws shall be subject to the revision and control of the Congress.

No state shall, without the consent of Congress, lay any duty of tonnage, keep troops, or ships of war in time of peace, enter into any agreement or compact with another state, or with a foreign power, or engage in war, unless actually invaded, or in such imminent danger as will not admit of delay.

Article II

Section 1. The executive power shall be vested in a President of the United States of America. He shall hold his office during the term of four years, and, together with the Vice President, chosen for the same term, be elected, as follows:

Each state shall appoint, in such manner as the Legislature thereof may direct, a number of electors, equal to the whole number of Senators and Representatives to which the State may be entitled in the Congress: but no Senator or Representative, or person holding an office of trust or profit under the United States, shall be appointed an elector.

The electors shall meet in their respective states, and vote by ballot for two persons, of whom one at least shall not be an inhabitant of the same state with themselves. And they shall make a list of all the persons voted for, and of the number of votes for each; which list they shall sign and certify, and transmit sealed to the seat of the government of the United States, directed to the President of the Senate. The President of the Senate shall, in the presence of the Senate and House of Representatives, open all the certificates, and the votes shall then be counted. The person having the greatest number of votes shall be the President, if such number be a majority of the whole number of electors appointed; and if there be more than one who have such majority, and have an equal number of votes, then the House of Representatives shall immediately choose by ballot one of them for President; and if no person have a majority, then from the five highest on the list the said House shall in like manner choose the President. But in choosing the President, the votes shall be taken by States, the representation from each state having one vote; A quorum for this purpose shall consist of a member or members from two thirds of the states, and a majority of all the states shall be necessary to a choice. In every case, after the choice of the President, the person having the greatest number of votes of the electors shall be the Vice President. But if there should remain two or more who have equal votes, the Senate shall choose from them by ballot the Vice President.

The Congress may determine the time of choosing the electors, and the day on which they shall give their votes; which day shall be the same throughout the United States.

No person except a natural born citizen, or a citizen of the United States, at the time of the adoption of this Constitution, shall be eligible to the office of President; neither shall any person be eligible to that office who shall not have attained to the age of thirty five years, and been fourteen Years a resident within the United States.

In case of the removal of the President from office, or of his death, resignation, or inability to discharge the powers and duties of the said office, the same shall devolve on the Vice President, and the Congress may by law provide for the case of removal, death, resignation or inability, both of the President and Vice President, declaring what officer shall then act as President, and such officer shall act accordingly, until the disability be removed, or a President shall be elected.

The President shall, at stated times, receive for his services, a compensation, which shall neither be increased nor diminished during the period for which he shall have been elected, and he shall not receive within that period any other emolument from the United States, or any of them.

Before he enter on the execution of his office, he shall take the following oath or affirmation:– "I do solemnly swear (or affirm) that I will faithfully execute the office of President of the United States, and will to the best of my ability, preserve, protect and defend the Constitution of the United States."

Section 2. The President shall be commander in chief of the Army and Navy of the United States, and of the militia of the several states, when called into the actual service of the United States; he may require the opinion, in writing, of the principal officer in each of the executive departments, upon any subject relating to the duties of their respective offices, and he shall have power to grant reprieves and pardons for offenses against the United States, except in cases of impeachment.

He shall have power, by and with the advice and consent of the Senate, to make treaties, provided two thirds of the Senators present concur; and he shall nominate, and by and with the advice and consent of the Senate, shall appoint ambassadors, other public ministers and consuls, judges of the Supreme Court, and all other officers of the United States, whose appointments are not herein otherwise provided for, and which shall be established by law: but the Congress may by law vest the appointment of such inferior officers, as they think proper, in the President alone, in the courts of law, or in the heads of departments.

The President shall have power to fill up all vacancies that may happen during the recess of the Senate, by granting commissions which shall expire at the end of their next session.

Section 3. He shall from time to time give to the Congress information of the state of the union, and recommend to their consideration such measures as he shall judge necessary and expedient; he may, on extraordinary occasions, convene both Houses, or either of them, and in case of disagreement between them, with respect to the time of adjournment, he may adjourn them to such time as he shall think proper; he shall receive ambassadors and other public ministers; he shall take care that the laws be faithfully executed, and shall commission all the officers of the United States.

Section 4. The President, Vice President and all civil officers of the United States, shall be removed from office on impeachment for, and conviction of, treason, bribery, or other high crimes and misdemeanors.

Article III

Section 1. The judicial power of the United States shall be vested in one Supreme Court and in such inferior courts as the Congress may from time to time ordain and establish. The judges, both of the supreme and inferior courts, shall hold their offices during good behaviour, and shall, at stated times, receive for their services, a compensation, which shall not be diminished during their continuance in office.

Section 2. The judicial power shall extend to all cases, in law and equity, arising under this Constitution, the laws of the United States, and treaties made, or which shall be made, under their authority;–to all cases affecting ambassadors, other public ministers and consuls;–to all cases of admiralty and maritime jurisdiction;–to controversies to which the United States shall be a party;–to controversies between two or more states;–between a state and citizens of another state;– between citizens of different states;–between citizens of the same state claiming lands under grants of different states, and between a state, or the citizens thereof, and foreign states, citizens or subjects.

In all cases affecting ambassadors, other public ministers and consuls, and those in which a state shall be party, the Supreme Court shall have original jurisdiction. In all the other cases before mentioned, the Supreme Court shall have appellate jurisdiction, both as to law and fact, with such exceptions, and under such regulations as the Congress shall make.

The trial of all crimes, except in cases of impeachment, shall

be by jury; and such trial shall be held in the state where the said crimes shall have been committed; but when not committed within any state, the trial shall be at such place or places as the Congress may by law have directed.

Section 3. Treason against the United States, shall consist only in levying war against them, or in adhering to their enemies, giving them aid and comfort. No person shall be convicted of treason unless on the testimony of two witnesses to the same overt act, or on confession in open court.

The Congress shall have power to declare the punishment of treason, but no attainder of treason shall work corruption of blood, or forfeiture except during the life of the person attainted.

Article IV

Section 1. Full faith and credit shall be given in each state to the public acts, records, and judicial proceedings of every other state. And the Congress may by general laws prescribe the manner in which such acts, records, and proceedings shall be proved, and the effect thereof.

Section 2. The citizens of each state shall be entitled to all privileges and immunities of citizens in the several states.

A person charged in any state with treason, felony, or other crime, who shall flee from justice, and be found in another state, shall on demand of the executive authority of the state from which he fled, be delivered up, to be removed to the state having jurisdiction of the crime.

No person held to service or labor in one state, under the laws thereof, escaping into another, shall, in consequence of any law or regulation therein, be discharged from such service or labor, but shall be delivered up on claim of the party to whom such service or labor may be due.

Section 3. New states may be admitted by the Congress into this union; but no new states shall be formed or erected within the jurisdiction of any other state; nor any state be formed by the junction of two or more states, or parts of states, without the consent of the legislatures of the states concerned as well as of the Congress.

The Congress shall have power to dispose of and make all needful rules and regulations respecting the territory or other property belonging to the United States; and nothing in this Constitution shall be so construed as to prejudice any claims of the United States, or of any particular state.

Section 4. The United States shall guarantee to every state in this union a republican form of government, and shall protect each of them against invasion; and on application of the legislature, or of the executive (when the legislature cannot be convened) against domestic violence.

Article V

The Congress, whenever two thirds of both houses shall deem it necessary, shall propose amendments to this Constitution, or, on the application of the legislatures of two thirds of the several states, shall call a convention for proposing amendments, which, in either case, shall be valid to all intents and purposes, as part of this Constitution, when ratified by the legislatures of three fourths of the several states, or by conventions in three fourths thereof, as the one or the other mode of ratification may be proposed by the Congress; provided that no amendment which may be made prior to the year one thousand eight hundred and eight shall in any manner affect the first and fourth clauses in the ninth section of the first article; and that no state, without its consent, shall be deprived of its equal suffrage in the Senate.

Article VI

All debts contracted and engagements entered into, before the adoption of this Constitution, shall be as valid against the United States under this Constitution, as under the Confederation.

This Constitution, and the laws of the United States which shall be made in pursuance thereof; and all treaties made, or which shall be made, under the authority of the United States, shall be the supreme law of the land; and the judges in every state shall be bound thereby, anything in the Constitution or laws of any State to the contrary notwithstanding.

The Senators and Representatives before mentioned, and the members of the several state legislatures, and all executive and judicial officers, both of the United States and of the several states, shall be bound by oath or affirmation, to support this Constitution; but no religious test shall ever be required as a qualification to any office or public trust under the United States.

Article VII

The ratification of the conventions of nine states shall be sufficient for the establishment of this Constitution between the states so ratifying the same.

Done in convention by the unanimous consent of the states present the seventeenth day of September in the year of our Lord one thousand seven hundred and eighty seven and of the independence of the United States of America the twelfth. In witness whereof We have hereunto subscribed our Names,

G. Washington-Presidt. and deputy from Virginia

New Hampshire: John Langdon, Nicholas Gilman

Massachusetts: Nathaniel Gorham, Rufus King

Connecticut: Wm: Saml. Johnson, Roger Sherman

New York: Alexander Hamilton

New Jersey: Wil: Livingston, David Brearly, Wm. Paterson, Jona: Dayton

Pennsylvania: B. Franklin, Thomas Mifflin, Robt. Morris, Geo. Clymer, Thos. FitzSimons, Jared Ingersoll, James Wilson, Gouv Morris

Delaware: Geo: Read, Gunning Bedford jun, John Dickinson, Richard Bassett, Jaco: Broom

Maryland: James McHenry, Dan of St Thos. Jenifer, Danl Carroll

Virginia: John Blair–, James Madison Jr.

North Carolina: Wm. Blount, Richd. Dobbs Spaight, Hu Williamson

South Carolina: J. Rutledge, Charles Cotesworth Pinckney, Charles Pinckney, Pierce Butler

Georgia: William Few, Abr Baldwin

http://www.billofrightsinstitute.org/Teach/freeResources/FoundingDocuments/Docs/Constitution.asp#Top

Accessed and Retrieved June 10, 2010

Amendment 1

Congress shall make no law respecting an establishment of religion, or prohibiting the free exercise thereof; or abridging the freedom of speech, or of the press; or the right of the people peaceably to assemble, and to petition the Government for a redress of grievances.

Amendment 2

A well regulated Militia, being necessary to the security of a free State, the right of the people to keep and bear Arms, shall not be infringed.

Amendment 3

No Soldier shall, in time of peace be quartered in any house, without the consent of the Owner, nor in time of war, but in a manner to be prescribed by law.

Amendment 4

The right of the people to be secure in their persons, houses, papers, and effects, against unreasonable searches and seizures, shall not be violated, and no Warrants shall issue, but upon probable cause, supported by Oath or affirmation, and particularly describing the place to be searched, and the persons or things to be seized.

Amendment 5

No person shall be held to answer for a capital, or otherwise infamous crime, unless on a presentment or indictment of a Grand Jury, except in cases arising in the land or naval forces, or in the Militia, when in actual service in time of War or public danger; nor shall any person be subject for the same offense to be twice put in jeopardy of life or limb; nor shall be compelled in any criminal case to be a witness against himself, nor be deprived of life, liberty, or property, without due process of law; nor shall private property be taken for public use, without just compensation.

Amendment 6

In all criminal prosecutions, the accused shall enjoy the right to a speedy and public trial, by an impartial jury of the State and district wherein the crime shall have been committed, which district shall have been previously ascertained by law, and to be informed of the nature and cause of the accusation; to be confronted with the witnesses against him; to have compulsory process for obtaining witnesses in his favor, and to have the Assistance of Counsel for his defence.

Amendment 7

In Suits at common law, where the value in controversy shall exceed twenty dollars, the right of trial by jury shall be preserved, and no fact tried by a jury, shall be otherwise re-examined in any Court of the United States, than according to the rules of the common law.

Amendment 8

Excessive bail shall not be required, nor excessive fines imposed, nor cruel and unusual punishments inflicted.

Amendment 9

The enumeration in the Constitution, of certain rights, shall not be construed to deny or disparage others retained by the people.

Amendment 10

The powers not delegated to the United States by the Constitution, nor prohibited by it to the States, are reserved to the States respectively, or to the people.

Amendment 11

The Judicial power of the United States shall not be construed to extend to any suit in law or equity, commenced or prosecuted against one of the United States by Citizens of another State, or by Citizens or Subjects of any Foreign State.

Amendment 12

The Electors shall meet in their respective states, and vote by ballot for President and Vice-President, one of whom, at least, shall not be an inhabitant of the same state with themselves; they shall name in their ballots the person voted for as President, and in distinct ballots the person voted for as Vice-President, and they shall make distinct lists of all persons voted for as President, and of all persons voted for as Vice-President and of the number of votes for each, which lists they shall sign and certify, and transmit sealed to the seat of the government of the United States, directed to the President of the Senate;

The President of the Senate shall, in the presence of the Senate and House of Representatives, open all the certificates and the votes shall then be counted;

The person having the greatest Number of votes for President, shall be the President, if such number be a majority of the whole number of Electors appointed; and if no person have such majority, then from the persons having the highest numbers not exceeding three on the list of those voted for as President, the House of Representatives shall choose immediately, by ballot, the President. But in choosing the President, the votes shall be taken by states, the representation from each state having one vote; a quorum for this purpose shall consist of a member or members from two-thirds of the states, and a majority of all the states shall be necessary to a choice. And if the House of Representatives shall not choose a President whenever the right of choice shall devolve upon them, before the fourth day of March next following, then the Vice-President shall act as President, as in the case of the death or other constitutional disability of the President.

The person having the greatest number of votes as Vice-President, shall be the Vice-President, if such number be a majority of the whole number of Electors appointed, and if no person have a majority, then from the two highest numbers on the list, the Senate shall choose the Vice-President; a quorum for the purpose shall consist of two-thirds of the whole number of Senators, and a majority of the whole number shall be necessary to a choice. But no person constitutionally ineligible to the office of President shall be eligible to that of Vice-President of the United States.

Amendment 13

1. Neither slavery nor involuntary servitude, except as a punishment for crime whereof the party shall have been duly convicted, shall exist within the United States, or any place subject to their jurisdiction.

2. Congress shall have power to enforce this article by appropriate legislation.

Amendment 14

1. All persons born or naturalized in the United States, and subject to the jurisdiction thereof, are citizens of the United States and of the State wherein they reside. No State shall make or enforce any law, which shall abridge the privileges or immunities of citizens of the United States; nor shall any State deprive any person of life, liberty, or property, without due process of law; nor deny to any person within its jurisdiction the equal protection of the laws.

2. Representatives shall be apportioned among the several States according to their respective numbers, counting the whole number of persons in each State, excluding Indians not taxed. But when the right to vote at any election for the choice of electors for President and Vice-President of the United States, Representatives in Congress, the Executive and Judicial officers of a State, or the members of the Legislature thereof, is denied to any of the male inhabitants of such State, being twenty-one years of age, and citizens of the United States, or in any way abridged, except for participation in rebellion, or other crime, the basis of representation therein shall be reduced in the proportion which the number of such male citizens shall bear to the whole number of male citizens twenty-one years of age in such State.

3. No person shall be a Senator or Representative in Congress, or elector of President and Vice-President, or hold any office, civil or military, under the United States, or under any State, who, having previously taken an oath, as a member of Congress, or as an officer of the United States, or as a member of any State legislature, or as an executive or judicial officer of any State, to support the Constitution of the United States, shall have engaged in insurrection or rebellion against the same, or given aid or comfort to the enemies thereof. But Congress may by a vote of two-thirds of each House, remove such disability.

4. The validity of the public debt of the United States, authorized by law, including debts incurred for payment of pensions and bounties for services in suppressing insurrection or rebellion, shall not be questioned. But neither the United States nor any State shall assume or pay any debt or obligation incurred in aid of insurrection or rebellion against the United States, or any claim for the loss or emancipation of any slave; but all such debts, obligations and claims shall be held illegal and void.

5. The Congress shall have power to enforce, by appropriate legislation, the provisions of this article.

Amendment 15

1. The right of citizens of the United States to vote shall not be denied or abridged by the United States or by any State on account of race, color, or previous condition of servitude.

2. The Congress shall have power to enforce this article by appropriate legislation.

Amendment 16

The Congress shall have power to lay and collect taxes on incomes, from whatever source derived, without apportionment among the several States, and without regard to any census or enumeration.

Amendment 17

The Senate of the United States shall be composed of two Senators from each State, elected by the people thereof, for six years; and each Senator shall have one vote. The electors in each State shall have the qualifications requisite for electors of the most numerous branch of the State legislatures.

When vacancies happen in the representation of any State in the Senate, the executive authority of such State shall issue writs of election to fill such vacancies: Provided, That the legislature of any State may empower the executive thereof to make temporary appointments until the people fill the vacancies by election as the legislature may direct.

This amendment shall not be so construed as to affect the election or term of any Senator chosen before it becomes valid as part of the Constitution.

Amendment 18

1. After one year from the ratification of this article the manufacture, sale, or transportation of intoxicating liquors within, the importation thereof into, or the exportation thereof from the United States and all territory subject to the jurisdiction thereof for beverage purposes is hereby prohibited.

2. The Congress and the several States shall have concurrent power to enforce this article by appropriate legislation.

3. This article shall be inoperative unless it shall have been ratified as an amendment to the Constitution by the legislatures of the several States, as provided in the Constitution, within seven years from the date of the submission hereof to the States by the Congress.

Amendment 19

The right of citizens of the United States to vote shall not be denied or abridged by the United States or by any State on account of sex.

Congress shall have power to enforce this article by appropriate legislation.

Amendment 20

1. The terms of the President and Vice President shall end at noon on the 20th day of January, and the terms of Senators and Representatives at noon on the 3rd day of January, of the years in which such terms would have ended if this article had not been ratified; and the terms of their successors shall then begin.

2. The Congress shall assemble at least once in every year, and such meeting shall begin at noon on the 3rd day of January, unless they shall by law appoint a different day.

3. If, at the time fixed for the beginning of the term of the President, the President elect shall have died, the Vice President elect shall become President. If a President shall not have been chosen before the time fixed for the beginning of his term, or if the President elect shall have failed to qualify, then the Vice President elect shall act as President until a President shall have qualified; and the Congress may by law provide for the case wherein neither a President elect nor a Vice President elect shall have qualified, declaring who shall then act as President, or the manner in which one who is to act shall be selected, and such person shall act accordingly until a President or Vice President shall have qualified.

4. The Congress may by law provide for the case of the death of any of the persons from whom the House of Representatives may choose a President whenever the right of choice shall have devolved upon them, and for the case of the death of any of the persons from whom the Senate may choose a Vice President whenever the right of choice shall have devolved upon them.

5. Sections 1 and 2 shall take effect on the 15th day of October following the ratification of this article.

6. This article shall be inoperative unless it shall have been ratified as an amendment to the Constitution by the legislatures of three-fourths of the several States within seven years from the date of its submission.

Amendment 21

1. The eighteenth article of amendment to the Constitution of the United States is hereby repealed.

2. The transportation or importation into any State, Territory, or possession of the United States for delivery or use therein of intoxicating liquors, in violation of the laws thereof, is hereby prohibited.

3. The article shall be inoperative unless it shall have been ratified as an amendment to the Constitution by conventions in the several States, as provided in the Constitution, within seven years from the date of the submission hereof to the States by the Congress.

Amendment 22

1. No person shall be elected to the office of the President more than twice, and no person who has held the office of President, or acted as President, for more than two years of a term to which some other person was elected President shall be elected to the office of the President more than once. But this Article shall not apply to any person holding the office of President, when this Article was proposed by the Congress, and shall not prevent any person who may be holding the office of President, or acting as President, during the term within which this Article becomes operative from holding the office of President or acting as President during the remainder of such term.

2. This article shall be inoperative unless it shall have been ratified as an amendment to the Constitution by the legislatures of three-fourths of the several States within seven years from the date of its submission to the States by the Congress.

Amendment 23

1. The District constituting the seat of Government of the United States shall appoint in such manner as the Congress may direct: A number of electors of President and Vice President equal to the whole number of Senators and Representatives in Congress to which the District would be entitled if it were a State, but in no event more than the least populous State; they shall be in addition to those appointed by the States, but they shall be considered, for the purposes of the election of President and Vice President, to be electors appointed by a State; and they shall meet in the District and perform such duties as provided by the twelfth article of amendment.

2. The Congress shall have power to enforce this article by appropriate legislation.

Amendment 24

1. The right of citizens of the United States to vote in any primary or other election for President or Vice President, for electors for President or Vice President, or for Senator or Representative in Congress, shall not be denied or abridged by the United States or any State by reason of failure to pay any poll tax or other tax.

2. The Congress shall have power to enforce this article by appropriate legislation.

Amendment 25

1. In case of the removal of the President from office or of his death or resignation, the Vice President shall become President.

2. Whenever there is a vacancy in the office of the Vice President, the President shall nominate a Vice President who shall take office upon confirmation by a majority vote of both Houses of Congress.

3. Whenever the President transmits to the President pro tempore of the Senate and the Speaker of the House of Representatives his written declaration that he is unable to discharge the powers and duties of his office, and until he transmits to them a written declaration to the contrary, such powers and duties shall be discharged by the Vice President as Acting President.

4. Whenever the Vice President and a majority of either the principal officers of the executive departments or of such other body as Congress may by law provide, transmit to the President pro tempore of the Senate and the Speaker of the House of Representatives their written declaration that the President is unable to discharge the powers and duties of his office, the Vice President shall immediately assume the powers and duties of the office as Acting President.

Thereafter, when the President transmits to the President pro tempore of the Senate and the Speaker of the House of Representatives his written declaration that no inability exists, he shall resume the powers and duties of his office unless the Vice President and a majority of either the principal officers of the executive department or of such other body as Congress may by law provide, transmit within four days to the President pro tempore of the Senate and the Speaker of the House of Representatives their written declaration that the President is unable to discharge the powers and duties of his office. Thereupon Congress shall decide the issue, assembling within forty eight hours for that purpose if not in session. If the Congress, within twenty one days after receipt of the latter written declaration, or, if Congress is not in session, within twenty one days after Congress is required to assemble, determines by two thirds vote of both Houses that the President is unable to discharge the powers and duties of his office, the Vice President shall continue to discharge the same as Acting President; otherwise, the President shall resume the powers and duties of his office.

Amendment 26

1. The right of citizens of the United States, who are eighteen years of age or older, to vote shall not be denied or abridged by the United States or by any State on account of age.

2. The Congress shall have power to enforce this article by appropriate legislation.

Amendment 27

No law, varying the compensation for the services of the Senators and Representatives, shall take effect, until an election of Representatives shall have intervened.

Accessed and Retrieved on June 10, 2010 http://www.usconstitution.net/const.txt

POLICIES, LAWS, AND LEGAL INFORMATION

Civil Rights Acts

Civil Rights Act of 1866, extending the rights of emancipated slaves
Civil Rights Act of 1871, also known as the Ku Klux Klan Act
Civil Rights Act of 1875, prohibiting discrimination in "public accommodations"; found unconstitutional in 1883
Civil Rights Act of 1957, establishing the Civil Rights Commission
Civil Rights Act of 1960, establishing federal inspection of local voter registration polls
Civil Rights Act of 1964, prohibiting discrimination based on race, color, religion, sex, and national origin by federal and state governments as well as some public places
Civil Rights Act of 1968, also known as the Fair Housing Act
Civil Rights Act of 1991, providing the right to trial by jury on discrimination limiting the amount that a jury could award

Disability Rights Laws

Titles VI and VII of the Civil Rights Act of 1964
Title IX of the Education Amendments of 1972

The following set of resources is taken from the U.S. Department of Justice Civil Rights Division Disability Rights Section, A Guide to Disability Rights Laws (www.ada.gov).

Americans with disabilities act of 1990. The ADA prohibits discrimination on the basis of disability in employment, State and local government, public accommodations, commercial facilities, transportation, and telecommunications. It also applies to the United States Congress.

To be protected by the ADA, one must have a disability or have a relationship or association with an individual with a disability. An individual with a disability is defined by the ADA as a person who has a physical or mental impairment that substantially limits one or more major life activities, a person who has a history or record of such an impairment, or a person who is perceived by others as having such an impairment. The ADA does not specifically name all of the impairments that are covered.

ADA title I: employment. Title I requires employers with 15 or more employees to provide qualified individuals with disabilities an equal opportunity to benefit from the full range of employment-related opportunities available to others. For example, it prohibits discrimination in recruitment, hiring, promotions, training, pay, social activities, and other privileges of employment. It restricts questions that can be asked about an applicant's disability before a job offer is made, and it requires that employers make reasonable accommodation to the known physical or mental limitations of otherwise qualified individuals with disabilities, unless it results in undue hardship. Religious entities with 15 or more employees are covered under title I.

ADA title II: state and local government activities. Title II covers all activities of State and local governments regardless of the government entity's size or receipt of Federal funding. Title II requires that State and local governments give people with disabilities an equal opportunity to benefit from all of their programs, services, and activities (e.g. public education, employment, transportation, recreation, health care, social services, courts, voting, and town meetings). State and local governments are required to follow specific architectural standards in the new construction and alteration of their buildings. They also must relocate programs or otherwise provide access in inaccessible older buildings, and communicate effectively with people who have hearing, vision, or speech disabilities. Public entities are not required to take actions that would result in undue financial and administrative burdens. They are required to make reasonable modifications to policies, practices, and procedures where necessary to avoid discrimination, unless they can demonstrate that doing so would fundamentally alter the nature of the service, program, or activity being provided.

ADA title II: public transportation. The transportation provisions of Title II cover public transportation services, such as city buses and public rail transit (e.g. subways, commuter rails, Amtrak). Public transportation authorities may not discriminate against people with disabilities in the provision of their services. They must comply with requirements for accessibility in newly purchased vehicles, make good faith efforts to purchase or lease accessible used buses, remanufacture buses in an accessible manner, and, unless it would result in an undue burden, provide paratransit where they operate fixed-route bus or rail systems. Paratransit is a service through which individuals who are unable to use the regular transit system independently (because of a physical or mental impairment) are picked up and dropped off at their destinations.

ADA title III: public accommodations. Title III covers businesses and nonprofit service providers that are public accommodations, privately operated entities offering certain types of courses and examinations, privately operated transportation, and commercial facilities. Public accommodations are private entities who own, lease, lease to, or operate facilities such as restaurants, retail stores, hotels, movie theaters, private schools, convention centers, doctors' offices, homeless shelters, transportation depots, zoos, funeral homes, day care centers, and recreation facilities including sports stadiums and fitness clubs. Transportation services provided by private entities are also covered by Title III.

Public accommodations must comply with basic nondiscrimination requirements that prohibit exclusion, segregation, and unequal treatment. They also must comply with specific requirements related to architectural standards for new and altered buildings; reasonable modifications to policies, practices, and procedures; effective communication with people with hearing, vision, or speech disabilities; and other access requirements. Additionally, public accommodations must remove barriers in existing buildings where it is easy to do so without much difficulty or expense, given the public accommodation's resources.

ADA title IV: telecommunications relay services. Title IV addresses telephone and television access for people with hearing and speech disabilities. It requires common carriers (telephone companies) to establish interstate and intrastate telecommunications relay services (TRS) 24 hours a day, 7 days a week. TRS enables callers with hearing and speech disabilities who use telecommunications devices for the deaf (TDDs), which are also known as teletypewriters (TTYs), and callers who use voice telephones to communicate with each other through a third party communications assistant. The Federal Communications Commission (FCC) has set minimum standards for TRS services. Title IV also requires closed captioning of Federally funded public service announcements.

Telecommunications act. Section 255 and Section 251(a)(2) of the Communications Act of 1934, as amended by the Telecommunications Act of 1996, require manufacturers of telecommunications equipment and providers of telecommunications services to ensure that such equipment and services are accessible to and usable by persons with disabilities, if readily achievable. These amendments ensure that people with disabilities will have access to a broad range of products and services such as telephones, cell phones, pagers, call-waiting, and operator services, that were often inaccessible to many users with disabilities.

Fair housing act. The Fair Housing Act, as amended in 1988, prohibits housing discrimination on the basis of race, color, religion, sex, disability, familial status, and national origin. Its coverage includes private housing, housing that receives Federal financial assistance, and State and local government housing. It is unlawful to discriminate in any aspect of selling or renting housing or to deny a dwelling to a buyer or renter because of the disability of that individual, an individual associated with the buyer or renter, or an individual who intends to live in the residence. Other covered activities include, for example, financing, zoning practices, new construction design, and advertising. The Fair Housing Act requires owners of housing facilities to make reasonable exceptions in their policies and operations to afford people with disabilities equal housing opportunities. For example, a landlord with a "no pets" policy may be required to grant an exception to this rule and allow an individual who is blind to keep a guide dog in the residence. The Fair Housing Act also requires landlords to allow tenants with disabilities to make reasonable access-related modifications to their private living space, as well as to common use spaces. (The landlord is not required to pay for the changes.) The Act further requires that new multifamily housing with four or more units be designed and built to allow access for persons with disabilities. This includes accessible common use areas, doors that are wide enough for wheelchairs, kitchens and bathrooms that allow a person using a wheelchair to maneuver, and other adaptable features within the units.

Air carrier access act. The Air Carrier Access Act prohibits discrimination in air transportation by domestic and foreign air carriers against qualified individuals with physical or mental impairments. It applies only to air carriers that provide regularly scheduled services for hire to the public. Requirements address a wide range of issues including boarding assistance and certain accessibility features in newly built aircraft and new or altered airport facilities. People may enforce rights under the Air Carrier Access Act by filing a complaint with the U.S. Department of Transportation, or by bringing a lawsuit in Federal court.

Voting accessibility for the elderly and handicapped act. The Voting Accessibility for the Elderly and Handicapped Act of 1984 generally requires polling places across the United States to be physically accessible to people with disabilities for federal elections. Where no accessible location is available to serve as a polling place, a political subdivision must provide an alternate means of casting a ballot on the day of the election. This law also requires states to make available registration and voting aids for disabled and elderly voters, including information by telecommunications devices for the deaf (TDDs) which are also known as teletypewriters (TTYs).

National voter registration act. The National Voter Registration Act of 1993, also known as the "Motor Voter Act," makes it easier for all Americans to exercise their fundamental right to vote. One of the basic purposes of the Act is to increase the historically low registration rates of minorities and persons with disabilities that have resulted from discrimination. The Motor Voter Act requires all offices of State-funded programs that are primarily engaged in providing services to persons with disabilities to provide all program applicants with voter registration forms, to assist them in completing the forms, and to transmit completed forms to the appropriate State official.

Civil rights of institutionalized persons act. The Civil Rights of Institutionalized Persons Act (CRIPA) authorizes the U.S. Attorney General to investigate conditions of confinement at State and local government institutions such as prisons, jails, pretrial detention centers, juvenile correctional facilities, publicly operated nursing homes, and institutions for people with psychiatric or developmental disabilities. Its purpose is to allow the Attorney General to uncover and correct widespread deficiencies that seriously jeopardize the health and safety of residents of institutions. The Attorney General does not have authority under CRIPA to investigate isolated incidents or to represent individual institutionalized persons.

The Attorney General may initiate civil law suits where there is reasonable cause to believe that conditions are "egregious or flagrant," that they are subjecting residents to "grievous harm," and that they are part of a "pattern or practice" of resistance to residents' full enjoyment of constitutional or Federal rights, including title II of the ADA and section 504 of the Rehabilitation Act.

Individuals with disabilities education act. The Individuals with Disabilities Education Act (IDEA) (formerly called P.L. 94–142 or the Education for all Handicapped Children Act of 1975) requires public schools to make available to all eligible children with disabilities a free appropriate public education in the least restrictive environment appropriate to their individual needs. IDEA requires public school systems to develop appropriate Individualized Education Programs (IEP's) for each child. The specific special education and related services outlined in each IEP reflect the individualized needs of each student. IDEA also mandates that particular procedures be followed in the development of the IEP. Each student's IEP must be developed by a team of knowledgeable persons and must be at least reviewed annually. The team includes the child's teacher; the parents, subject to certain limited exceptions; the child, if determined appropriate; an agency representative who is qualified to provide or supervise the provision of special education; and other individuals at the parents' or agency's discretion. If parents disagree with the proposed IEP, they can request a due process hearing and a review from the State educational agency if applicable in that state. They also can appeal the State agency's decision to State or Federal court.

Rehabilitation act. The Rehabilitation Act prohibits discrimination on the basis of disability in programs conducted by Federal agencies, in programs receiving Federal financial assistance, in Federal employment, and in the employment practices of Federal contractors. The standards for determining employment discrimination under the Rehabilitation Act are the same as those used in title I of the Americans with Disabilities Act.

Section 501. Section 501 requires affirmative action and nondiscrimination in employment by Federal agencies of the executive branch. To obtain more information or to file a complaint, employees should contact their agency's Equal Employment Opportunity Office.

Section 503. Section 503 requires affirmative action and prohibits employment discrimination by Federal government contractors and subcontractors with contracts of more than $10,000.

Section 504. Section 504 states that "no qualified individual with a disability in the United States shall be excluded from, denied the benefits of, or be subjected to discrimination under" any program or activity that either receives Federal financial assistance or is conducted by any Executive agency or the United States Postal Service. Each Federal agency has its own set of section 504 regulations that apply to its own programs. Agencies that provide Federal financial assistance also have section 504 regulations covering entities that receive Federal aid. Requirements common to these regulations include reasonable accommodation for employees with disabilities; program accessibility; effective communication with people who have hearing or vision disabilities; and accessible new construction and alterations. Each agency is responsible for enforcing its own regulations. Section 504 may also be enforced through private lawsuits. It is not necessary to file a complaint with a Federal agency or to receive a "right-to-sue" letter before going to court.

Section 508. Section 508 establishes requirements for electronic and information technology developed, maintained, procured, or used by the Federal government. Section 508 requires Federal electronic and information technology to be accessible to people with disabilities, including employees and members of the public. An accessible information technology system is one that can be operated in a variety of ways and does not rely on a single sense or ability of the user. For example, a system that provides output only in visual format may not be accessible to people with visual impairments and a system that provides output only in audio format may not be accessible to people who are deaf or hard of hearing. Some individuals with disabilities may need accessibility-related software or peripheral devices in order to use systems that comply with Section 508.

Architectural barriers act. The Architectural Barriers Act (ABA) requires that buildings and facilities that are designed, constructed, or altered with Federal funds, or leased by a Federal agency, comply with Federal standards for physical accessibility. ABA requirements are limited to architectural standards in new and altered buildings and in newly leased facilities. They do not address the activities conducted in those buildings and facilities. Facilities of the U.S. Postal Service are covered by the ABA.

STATUTE CITATIONS

Air Carrier Access Act of 1986
49 U.S.C. § 41705
Implementing regulation:
14 CFR Part 382

Americans with Disabilities Act of 1990
42 U.S.C. §§ 12101 et seq.
Implementing regulations:
29 CFR Parts 1630, 1602 (Title I, EEOC)
28 CFR Part 35 (Title II, Department of Justice)
49 CFR Parts 27, 37, 38 (Title II, III, Department of Transportation)
28 CFR Part 36 (Title III, Department of Justice)
47 CFR §§ 64.601 et seq. (Title IV, FCC)

Architectural Barriers Act of 1968
42 U.S.C. §§ 4151 et seq.
Implementing regulation:
41 CFR Subpart 101-19.6

Civil Rights of Institutionalized Persons Act
42 U.S.C. §§ 1997 et seq.

Fair Housing Amendments Act of 1988
42 U.S.C. §§ 3601 et seq.
Implementing regulation:
24 CFR Parts 100 et seq.

Individuals with Disabilities Education Act
20 U.S.C. §§ 1400 et seq.
Implementing regulation:
34 CFR Part 300

National Voter Registration Act of 1993
42 U.S.C. §§ 1973gg et seq.

Section 501 of the Rehabilitation Act of 1973, as amended
29 U.S.C. § 791
Implementing regulation:
29 CFR § 1614.203

Section 503 of the Rehabilitation Act of 1973, as amended
29 U.S.C. § 793
Implementing regulation:
41 CFR Part 60-741

Section 504 of the Rehabilitation Act of 1973, as amended
29 U.S.C. § 794
Over 20 implementing regulations for federally assisted programs, including:
34 CFR Part 104 (Department of Education)
45 CFR Part 84 (Department of Health and Human Services)
28 CFR §§ 42.501 et seq.

Over 95 implementing regulations for federally conducted programs, including:
28 CFR Part 39 (Department of Justice)

Section 508 of the Rehabilitation Act of 1973, as amended
29 U.S.C. § 794d
Telecommunications Act of 1996
47 U.S.C. §§ 255, 251(a)(2)
Voting Accessibility for the Elderly and Handicapped Act of 1984
42 U.S.C. §§ 1973ee et seq.

FAMOUS FIRST AFRICAN AMERICAN FACTS

African American Firsts: Government

Local elected official: John Mercer Langston, 1855, town clerk of Brownhelm Township, Ohio.
State elected official: Alexander Lucius Twilight, 1836, the Vermont legislature.
Mayor of major city: Carl Stokes, Cleveland, Ohio, 1967–1971.
first Black woman to serve as a mayor of a major U.S. city: Sharon Pratt Dixon Kelly, Washington, DC, 1991–1995.
Governor (appointed): P.B.S. Pinchback served as governor of Louisiana from Dec. 9, 1872–Jan. 13, 1873, during impeachment proceedings against the elected governor.
Governor (elected): L. Douglas Wilder, Virginia, 1990–1994. The only other elected Black governor has been Deval Patrick, Massachusetts, 2007–present
U.S. Representative: Joseph Rainey became a Congressman from South Carolina in 1870 and was re-elected four more times.
The first Black female U.S. Representative was Shirley Chisholm, Congresswoman from New York, 1969–1983.
U.S. Senator: Hiram Revels became Senator from Mississippi from Feb. 25, 1870, to March 4, 1871, during Reconstruction.
Edward Brooke became the first African American Senator since Reconstruction, 1966–1979.
Carol Mosely Braun became the first Black woman Senator serving from 1992–1998 for the state of Illinois. (There have only been a total of five Black senators in U.S. history: The remaining three are Blanche K. Bruce (1875–1881), Barack Obama (2005–2008), and Roland Burris (2009–)
U.S. cabinet member: Robert C. Weaver, 1966–1968, Secretary of the Department of Housing and Urban Development under Lyndon Johnson.
The first Black female cabinet secretary was Patricia Harris, 1977, Secretary of the Department of Housing and Urban Development under Jimmy Carter.
U.S. Secretary of State: Gen. Colin Powell, 2001–2004.
The first Black female Secretary of State was Condoleezza Rice, 2005–2009.
Major Party Nominee for President: Sen. Barack Obama, 2008. The Democratic Party selected him as its presidential nominee.

U.S. President: Barack Obama. Obama defeated Sen. John McCain in the general election on November 4, 2008, and was inaugurated as the 44th president of the United States on January 20, 2009.

African American Firsts: Law

Editor, Harvard Law Review: Charles Hamilton Houston, 1919.
Barack Obama became the first president of the Harvard Law Review.
Federal Judge: William Henry Hastie, 1946.
Constance Baker Motley became the first Black woman federal judge, 1966.
U.S. Supreme Court Justice: Thurgood Marshall, 1967–1991.
Clarence Thomas became the second African American to serve on the Court in 1991.

African American Firsts: Diplomacy

U.S. diplomat: Ebenezer D. Bassett, 1869, became minister-resident to Haiti;
Patricia Harris became the first Black female ambassador (1965; Luxembourg).
U.S. Representative to the UN: Andrew Young (1977–1979).
Nobel Peace Prize winner: Ralph J. Bunche received the prize in 1950 for mediating the Arab-Israeli truce.
Martin Luther King, Jr. became the second African American Peace Prize winner in 1964.
President Barack Obama became the third African American and first United States sitting President to win the Nobel Peace Prize in 2009.

African American Firsts: Military

Combat pilot: Georgia-born Eugene Jacques Bullard, 1917, denied entry into the U.S. Army Air Corps because of his race, served throughout World War I in the French Flying Corps. He received the Legion of Honor, France's highest honor, among many other decorations.
First Congressional Medal of Honor winner: Sgt. William H. Carney for bravery during the Civil War. He received his Congressional Medal of Honor in 1900.
General: Benjamin O. Davis, Sr., 1940–1948.
Chairman of the Joint Chiefs of Staff: Colin Powell, 1989–1993.

African American Firsts: Science and Medicine

First patent holder: Thomas L. Jennings, 1821, for a dry-cleaning process.
Sarah E. Goode, 1885, became the first African-American woman to receive a patent, for a bed that folded up into a cabinet.
M.D. degree: James McCune Smith, 1837, University of Glasgow.
Rebecca Lee Crumpler became the first Black woman to receive an M.D. degree. She graduated from the New England Female Medical College in 1864.
Inventor of the blood bank: Dr. Charles Drew, 1940.
Heart surgery pioneer: Daniel Hale Williams, 1893.

First astronaut: Robert H. Lawrence, Jr., 1967, was the first Black astronaut, but he died in a plane crash during a training flight and never made it into space.
Guion Bluford, 1983, became the first Black astronaut to travel in space.
Mae Jemison, 1992, became the first Black female astronaut.
Frederick D. Gregory, 1998, was the first African American shuttle commander.

African American Firsts: Scholarship

College graduate (B.A.): Alexander Lucius Twilight, 1823, Middlebury College.
First Black woman to receive a B.A. degree: Mary Jane Patterson, 1862, Oberlin College.
Ph.D.: Edward A. Bouchet, 1876, received a Ph.D. from Yale University.
In 1921, three individuals became the first U.S. Black women to earn Ph.D's: Georgiana Simpson, University of Chicago; Sadie Tanner Mossell Alexander, University of Pennsylvania; and Eva Beatrice Dykes, Radcliffe College.
Rhodes Scholar: Alain L. Locke, 1907.
College president: Daniel A. Payne, 1856, Wilberforce University, Ohio.
Ivy League president: Ruth Simmons, 2001, Brown University.

African American Firsts: Literature

Novelist: Harriet Wilson, Our Nig (1859).
Poet: Lucy Terry, 1746, "Bar's Fight." It is her only surviving poem.
Poet (published): Phillis Wheatley, 1773, Poems on Various Subjects, Religious and Moral. Considered the founder of African American literature.
Pulitzer Prize winner in Poetry: Gwendolyn Brooks, 1950.
Pulitzer Prize winner in Drama: Charles Gordone, 1970, for his play, No Place To Be Somebody.
Nobel Prize for Literature winner: Toni Morrison, 1993.
Poet Laureate: Robert Hayden, 1976–1978
First Black woman Poet Laureate: Rita Dove, 1993–1995.

African American Firsts: Music and Dance

Member of the New York City Opera: Todd Duncan, 1945.
Member of the Metropolitan Opera Company: Marian Anderson, 1955.
Male Grammy Award winner: Count Basie, 1958.
Female Grammy Award winner: Ella Fitzgerald, 1958.
Principal dancer in a major dance company: Arthur Mitchell, 1959, New York City Ballet.

African American Firsts: Film

First Oscar: Hattie McDaniel, 1940, supporting actress, *Gone with the Wind.*
Oscar, Best Actor/Actress: Sidney Poitier, 1963, *Lilies of the Field*; Halle Berry, 2001, *Monster's Ball.*

Oscar, Best Actress Nominee: Dorothy Dandridge, 1954, *Carmen Jones.*
Film director: Oscar Micheaux, 1919, wrote, directed, and produced *The Homesteader,* a feature film.
Hollywood director: Gordon Parks directed and wrote *The Learning Tree* for Warner Brothers in 1969.

African American Firsts: Television

Network television show host: Nat King Cole, 1956, "The Nat King Cole Show"
Oprah Winfrey became the first Black woman television host in 1986, "The Oprah Winfrey Show."
Star of a network television show: Bill Cosby, 1965, "I Spy".

African American Firsts: Sports

Major league baseball player: Jackie Robinson, 1947, Brooklyn Dodgers.
Elected to the Baseball Hall of Fame: Jackie Robinson, 1962.
NFL quarterback: Willie Thrower, 1953.
NFL football coach: Fritz Pollard, 1922–1937.
Golf champion: Tiger Woods, 1997, won the Masters Golf Tournament.
NHL hockey player: Willie O'Ree, 1958, Boston Bruins.
World cycling champion: Marshall W. "Major" Taylor, 1899.
Tennis champion: Althea Gibson became the first Black person to play in and win Wimbledon and the United States national tennis championship. She won both tournaments twice, in 1957 and 1958. In all, Gibson won 56 tournaments, including five Grand Slam singles events. The first Black male champion was Arthur Ashe, who won the 1968 U.S. Open, the 1970 Australian Open, and the 1975 Wimbledon championship.
Heavyweight boxing champion: Jack Johnson, 1908.
Olympic medalist (Summer Games): George Poage, 1904, won two bronze medals in the 200m hurdles and 400mm hurdles.
Olympic gold medalist (Summer Games): John Baxter "Doc" Taylor, 1908, won a gold medal as part of the 4 x 400 m relay team.
Olympic gold medalist (Summer Games; individual): DeHart Hubbard, 1924, for the long jump; the first woman was Alice Coachman, who won the high jump in 1948.
Olympic medalist (Winter Games): Debi Thomas, 1988, won the bronze in figure skating.
Olympic gold medalist (Winter Games): Vonetta Flowers, 2002, bobsled.
Olympic gold medalist (Winter Games; individual): Shani Davis, 2006, 1,000 meter speedskating.

Other African American Firsts

Licensed Pilot: Bessie Coleman, 1921.
Millionaire: Madame C. J. Walker.

Billionaire: Robert Johnson, 2001, former owner of Black Entertainment Television; Oprah Winfrey, owner of Harpo Studios and the Oprah Winfrey Show, 2003.

Portrayal on a postage stamp: Booker T. Washington, 1940 (and also 1956).

Miss America: Vanessa Williams, 1984, representing New York. When controversial photos surfaced and Williams resigned, Suzette Charles, the runner-up, also an African American, assumed the title. She represented New Jersey. Three additional African Americans have been Miss Americas: Debbye Turner (1990), Marjorie Vincent (1991), and Kimberly Aiken (1994).

Explorer, North Pole: Matthew A. Henson, 1909, accompanied Robert E. Peary on the first successful U.S. expedition to the North Pole.

Explorer, South Pole: George Gibbs, 1939–1941 accompanied Richard Byrd.

Flight around the world: Barrington Irving, 2007, from Miami Gardens, Florida, flew a Columbia 400 plane named Inspiration around the world in 96 days, 150 hours (March 23–June 27).

Accessed and Retrieved June 11, 2010 http://www.infoplease.com/spot/bhmfirsts.html

FAMOUS FIRST HISPANIC AMERICAN FACTS

Hispanic American Firsts: Government

Member of U.S. Congress: Joseph Marion Hernández, 1822, delegate from the Florida territory.

U.S. Representative: Romualdo Pacheco, a representative from California, was elected in 1876 by a one-vote margin. He served for four months before his opponent succeeded in contesting the results. In 1879, he was again elected to Congress, where he served for two terms.

U.S. Senator: Octaviano Larrazolo was elected in 1928 to finish the term of New Mexico senator Andieus Jones, who had died in office. He served for six months before falling ill and stepping down; he died in 1930.

The first Hispanic senator to serve an entire term (and then some) was Dennis Chávez, of New Mexico, who served from 1935 through 1962.

Administrator of the Federal Aviation Agency: General Elwood "Pete" Quesada helped create this agency to manage the growing aviation field and improve airline safety. He served in this position from 1958 to 1961. The agency became the Federal Aviation Administration in 1966.

U.S. Treasurer: Romana Acosta Bañuelos, 1971–1974.

U.S. cabinet member: Lauro F. Cavazos, 1988–1990, Secretary of Education.

U.S. Surgeon General: Antonia Coello Novello, 1990–1993. She was also the first woman ever to hold the position.

U.S. Secretary of Transportation: Federico Peña, 1993.

U.S. Secretary of Housing and Urban Development: Henry Cisneros, 1993.

U.S. Attorney General: Alberto Gonzales, 2005.

Democrat to run for President: Bill Richardson, 2008. Though he eventually lost the nomination to Barack Obama, Richardson made history by entering the race.

U.S. Supreme Court Justice: Sonia Sotomayor, 2009. She was also the third woman to hold the position.

Hispanic American Firsts: Military

Flying ace: Col. Manuel J. Fernández, Jr., who flew 125 combat missions in the Korean War.

Medal of Honor recipient: Philip Bazaar, a Chilean member of the U.S. Navy, for bravery during the Civil War. He received his Congressional Medal of Honor in 1865.

Admiral, U.S. Navy: David G. Farragut. In 1866, he became the first U.S. naval officer ever to be awarded the rank of admiral. The first Hispanic American to become a four-star admiral was Horacio Rivero of Puerto Rico, in 1964.

General, U.S. Army: Richard E. Cavazos, 1976. In 1982, he became the Army's first Hispanic four-star general.

Secretary of the Navy: Edward Hidalgo, 1979.

Hispanic American Firsts: Science and Medicine

Astronaut: Franklin Chang-Dìaz, 1986. He flew on a total of seven space-shuttle missions.

The first female Hispanic astronaut was Ellen Ochoa, whose first of four shuttle missions was in 1991.

Nobel Prize in Physics: Luiz Walter Alvarez, 1968, for discoveries about subatomic particles. Later, he and his son proposed the now-accepted theory that the mass dinosaur extinction was caused by a meteor impact.

Nobel Prize in Physiology or Medicine: Severo Ochoa, 1959, for the synthesis of ribonucleic acid (RNA).

Hispanic American Firsts: Literature

Novel in English, written and published in U.S.: María Amparo Ruiz de Burton, *Who Would Have Thought It?* (1872). She's better known for her 1885 second novel, *The Squatter and the Don.*

Pulitzer Prize for Fiction: Oscar Hijuelos, 1990, for his novel *The Mambo Kings Play Songs of Love.*

Pulitzer Prize for Drama: Nilo Cruz, 2003, for his play *Anna in the Tropics.*

Hispanic American Firsts: Music

Opera diva: Lucrezia Bori, who debuted at the Metropolitan Opera in 1912.

Rock star: Richie Valens, 1958.

Rock & Roll Hall of Fame inductee: Carlos Santana, 1998.

Hispanic American Firsts: Film

Oscar, Best Actor: José Ferrer, 1950, *Cyrano de Bergerac.*

Oscar, Best Supporting Actress: Rita Moreno, 1961, *West Side Story.*

Oscar, Best Supporting Actor: Anthony Quinn, 1952, *Viva Zapata!*.
Hollywood director: Raoul Walsh, 1914, *The Life of General Villa*.
Matinee idol: Ramón Navarro, 1923, *The Prisoner of Zenda*.
Leading lady: Dolores del Río, 1925, *Joanne*.

Hispanic American Firsts: *Drama*

Tony, Best Director: José Quintero, 1973.
Tony, Best Supporting Actress: Rita Moreno, 1975, *The Ritz*. In 1977, Moreno became the first Hispanic American (and the second person ever) to have won an Oscar, a Grammy, a Tony, and an Emmy, picking up the last of those for her performance as guest host on *The Muppet Show*.

Hispanic American Firsts: *Television*

Star of a network television show: Desi Arnaz, 1952, *I Love Lucy*.
Broadcaster of the Year: Geraldo Rivera, 1971.

Hispanic American Firsts: *Baseball*

Major league player: Esteban Bellán, 1871, Troy Haymakers.
World Series player: Adolfo "Dolf" Luque, 1919, relief pitcher for the Cincinnati Reds, against the infamous "Black Sox." (He later pitched for the New York Giants in the 1933 Series and was credited with the win in the final game.)
All-Star Game player: Alfonso "Chico" Carrasquel, 1951, starting shortstop for the American League.
Rookie of the Year: Luis Aparicio, 1956, shortstop, Chicago White Sox.
No-hitter: Juan Marichal, June 15, 1963, for the San Francisco Giants, against the Houston Colt .45s.
Hall of Fame inductee: Roberto Clemente, 1973. He was also the first Hispanic player to serve on the Players Association Board and to reach 3,000 hits.
Team owner: Arturo "Arte" Moreno bought the Anaheim Angels in 2003, becoming the first Hispanic owner of any major U.S. sports franchise. In 2005, he renamed it the Los Angeles Angels of Anaheim.

Hispanic American Firsts: *Football*

NFL player: Ignacio "Lou" Molinet, 1927.
NFL draft pick: Joe Aguirre, 1941.
Starting NFL quarterback: Tom Flores, 1960.
#1 NFL draft pick: Jim Plunkett, 1971.
Football Hall of Fame inductee: Tom Fears, 1970. He also became the first Hispanic American head coach in 1967.

Hispanic American Firsts: Other Sports

Grand Slam championship winner: Richard "Pancho" González, 1948.
LPGA Hall of Fame inductee: Nancy López, 1987. In 1978, she became the first player to have won the Rookie of the Year Award, Player of the Year Award, and Vare Trophy in the same season.
Heavyweight boxing champ: John Ruiz, 2001, defeating Evander Holyfield.
NHL 1st-round draft pick: Scott Gomez, 1998.

Other Hispanic American Firsts

Supermodel: Christy Turlington.
Labor leader: Juan Gómez, 1883. The first female Hispanic labor leader of note was Lucy González Parsons, 1886.
Entertainer on the cover of TIME magazine: Joan Baez, 1962.
Accessed and Retrieved June 11, 2010 http://www.infoplease.com/ipa/A0933896.html

FAMOUS FIRST ASIAN AMERICAN FACTS

Asian American Firsts: Government

U.S. Representative: Dalip Singh Saund, 1956, representative from California.
The first female Asian American elected to Congress was Patsy Takemoto Mink, elected in 1964 as a representative from Hawaii.
U.S. Senator: Hiram Fong, 1959, one of Hawaii's first two senators.
Federal court judge: Herbert Choy, 1971, appointed to the U.S. court of appeals for the ninth circuit.
U.S. ambassador: Julia Chang Bloch, 1989, appointed ambassador to the Kingdom of Nepal.
State legislator: Wing F. Ong, 1946, elected to the Arizona House of Representatives.
Governor: George R. Ariyoshi, 1974, governor of Hawaii.
The first on the mainland was Gary Locke, elected governor of Washington in 1996.
Mayor of a major U.S. city: Norman Yoshio Mineta, 1971, in San Jose, California.
Member of presidential cabinet: Norman Yoshio Mineta, 2000, appointed Secretary of Commerce. In 2001, he became the first cabinet member to switch directly from a Democratic to Republican cabinet—becoming Secretary of Transportation—and the only Democrat in George W. Bush's cabinet.
The first female Asian American cabinet member was Elaine Chao, appointed Secretary of Labor in 2001.
Vietnamese American member of Congress: Anh Cao won a special election for a seat in the House of Representatives, representing New Orleans, Louisiana, in December 2008.

Asian American Firsts: Aviation

Female aviator: Katherine Sui Fun Cheung, licensed in 1932.
Astronaut (in space): Ellison Onizuka, first spaceflight in 1985. Died in the 1986 Challenger disaster.

Asian American Firsts: Science and Medicine

Isolated epinephrine (adrenaline) from the suprarenal gland: Jokichi Takamine, 1901.
Invented pulse transfer controlling device leading to magnetic core memory: An Wang, 1949.
Cloned the AIDS virus: Flossie Wong-Staal, 1984.

Asian American Firsts: Film and Television

Movie star: Anna May Wong, who starred in the 1921 film *Bits of Life* and many other movies.
Academy Award winner: Haing Ngor, Best Supporting Actor of 1984 for his role in *The Killing Fields*
Host of own network TV series: Anna May Wong, 1951, *The Gallery of Madame Liu Tsong.*
Star of own network sitcom: Pat Morita, 1976, *Mr. T and Tina.*

Asian American Firsts: News Reporting

First network news reporters: Ken Kashiwahara and Connie Chung, 1974. In 1993, Chung became the first Asian American to be a nightly news anchor for a major network (CBS).
First anchor of a national radio program: Emil Guillermo, 1989, host of NPR's *All Things Considered.*

Asian American Firsts: Other

First to command a combat battalion: Young Oak Kim, of the 100th Infantry Battalion, 1943.
First selected in the first round of NFL draft: Eugene Chung, 1992, selected by New England.
(Author: Shmuel Ross)
Accessed and Retrieved June 11, 2010 http://www.infoplease.com/spot/apahmfirsts.html

REFERENCES

Banks, J. A. (1973). *Teaching ethnic studies: Concepts and strategies.* Washington, DC: National Council for the Social Studies.

Banks, J. A. (1995). Multicultural education: Historical development, dimensions, and practice. In J. A. Banks & C. A. M. Banks (Eds.), *Handbook of research on multicultural education* (pp. 3–24). New York: Macmillan.

Banks, J. A. (Ed.). (1996). *Multicultural education, transformative knowledge, and action: Historical and contemporary perspectives.* New York: Teachers College Press.

Banks, J. A. (1997). *Educating citizens in a multicultural society.* Multicultural Education Series. New York: Teachers College Press.

Banks, J. A., & Banks, C. A. M. (1995). Equity pedagogy: An essential component of multicultural education. *Theory into Practice, 34,* 152–158.

Banks, J. A., & Banks, C. A. M. (Eds.). (2001). *Handbook of research on multicultural education.* San Francisco: Jossey-Bass.

Berger, J. (1977). *Ways of seeing.* New York: Penguin Books.

Bonilla-Silva, E. (2006). *Racism without racists: Color-blind racism and the persistence of racial inequality in the United States* (2nd ed.). Boulder, CO: Rowman & Littlefield Publishers, Inc.

Case, M. A. C. (1995). Disaggregating gender from sex and sexual orientation: The effeminate man in the law and feminist jurisprudence. *Yale Law Journal, 105,* 1–105.

Carlson, D. (1998). Finding a voice, and losing your way! *Educational Theory, 48*(4), 541–554.

Carlson, D., & Apple, M. (Eds.). (1998). *Power, knowledge, pedagogy: The meaning of democratic education in unsettling times.* Colorado, CO: Westview Press.

Carlson, D., & Gause, C. P. (2007). *Keeping the promise: Essays on leadership, democracy, and education.* New York: Peter Lang.

Cooper, C.W., & Gause, C. P. (2007). "Who's afraid of the big bad wolf?": Facing identity politics and resistance when teaching for social justice. In D. Carlson, & C. P. Gause (Eds.), *Keeping the promise: Essays on leadership, democracy and education.* New York: Peter Lang.

Delpit, L. (1995). *Other people's children: Cultural conflict in the classroom.* New York: New Press.

DuBois, W. E. B. (1903). *The souls of black folk.* Illinois, IL: A.C. McClurg & Co.

Eskridge, W. N., Jr. (2000). No promo homo: The sedimentation of antigay discourse and the channelling effect of judicial review. *New York University Law Review, 75,* 1327–1411.

Foster, M. (1997). *Black teachers on teaching.* New York: The New Press.

Franke, K. M. (1995). The central mistake of sex discrimination law: The disaggregation of sex from gender. *University of Pennsylvania Law Review, 144,* 1–99.

Freire, P. (1970). *Pedagogy of the oppressed.* New York: Continuum.

Freire, P. (1998). *Pedagogy of freedom: Ethics, democracy, and civic courage.* Lanham, MD: Rowman & Littlefield.

Gause, C. P. (2001). *How African American educators "make-sense" of Hip Hop culture in today's public schools: A case study.* Unpublished dissertation, Miami University.

Gause, C. P. (2005a). The ghetto sophisticates: Performing black masculinity, saving lost souls and serving as leaders of the New School. *Taboo: The Journal of Culture and Education, 9*(1), 17–31.

Gause, C. P. (2005b). Navigating the stormy seas: Critical perspectives on the intersection of popular culture and educational leader-"ship". *Journal of School Leadership, 15*(3), 333–342.

Gause, C. P. (2005c). Guest editor's introduction: Edu-tainment: Popular culture in the making of schools for the 21st century. *Journal of School Leadership, 15*(3), 240–242.

Gause, C. P. (2008). *Integration matters: Navigating identity, culture and resistance.* New York: Peter Lang.

Gause, C. P. (2009). *201+ strategies for transforming today's schools: A resource guide for educational leaders, school administrators, teachers, parents, and students.* Maine, ME: Booklocker.com.

REFERENCES

Gause, C. P., Reitzug, U. C., & Villaverde, L. E. (2007). Beyond generic democracy: Holding our students accountable for democratic leadership and practice. In D. Carlson, & C. P. Gause (Eds.), *Keeping the promise: Essays on leadership, democracy and education.* New York: Peter Lang.

Gay, G. (2000). *Culturally responsive teaching: Theory, research and practice.* New York: Teachers College Press.

Giroux, H. A. (1995). Is there a place for cultural studies in colleges of education? In H. A. Giroux, C. Lankshear, P. McLaren, & M. Peters (Eds.), *Counternarratives: Cultural studies and critical pedagogies in postmodern spaces* (pp. 41–58). New York: Routledge.

Gollnick, D., & Chinn, P. (2009). *Multicultural education in a pluralistic society.* New Jersey, NJ: Merrill.

Gutmann, A., & Thompson, D. (1996). *Democracy and disagreement.* Cambridge, MA: Harvard University Press.

Hamilton, K. (2002). Race in the college classroom. *Black Issues in Higher Education, 19*(2), 32–36.

hooks, b. (1994). *Teaching to transgress: Education as the practice of freedom.* New York: Routledge.

hooks, b. (2003). *Teaching community. A Pedagogy of hope.* New York: Routledge.

hooks, b. (2004). *We real cool. Black men and masculinity.* New York: Routledge.

Hopkins, R. (1997). *Educating black males: Critical lessons in schooling, community, and power.* Albany, NY: State University of New York Press.

Kincheloe, J. (2008). *Critical pedagogy primer.* New York: Peter Lang.

Kincheloe, J., & Steinberg, S. (1997). *Changing multiculturalism: New times, new curriculum.* London: Open University Press.

Kincheloe, J., Steinberg, S., Rodriguez, N., & Chennault, R. (Eds.). (1998). *White reign: Deploying whiteness in America.* New York: St. Martin's Press.

Knight, T., & Pearl, A. (2000). Democratic education and critical pedagogy. *The Urban Review, 32*(3), 197–226.

Kozol, J. (1992). *Savage inequalities: Children in America's schools.* New York: Harper.

Ladson-Billings, G. J. (1997). *The dreamkeepers: Successful teachers of African-American children.* San Francisco: Jossey-Bass.

Ladson-Billings, G. J. (2001). *Crossing over to Canaan: The journey of new teachers in diverse classrooms.* San Francisco: Josses-Bass.

Ladson-Billings, G. J. (2005). *Beyond the big house: African American educators on teacher education.* New York: Teachers College Press.

Lindsey, R., Robins, K. N., & Terrell, R. (1999). *Cultural proficiency: A manual for school leaders.* Thousand Oaks, CA: Corwin Press.

Lopez, G. R. (2003). The (racially-neutral) politics of education: A critical race theory perspective. *Educational Administrative Quarterly, 39*(1), 68–94.

McGregor, J. (1993). Effectiveness of role playing and antiracist teaching in reducing student prejudice. *Journal of Educational Research, 86*(4): 215–226.

Miller, N. (1995). *Out of the past: Gay and lesbian history from 1869 to the present.* New York: Vintage Press.

Nagda, B. A., Gurin, P., & Lopze, G. E. (2003). Transformative pedagogy for democracy and social justice. *Race, Ethnicity and Education, 6*(2), 165–191.

Palmer, P. J. (1998). *The courage to teach: Exploring the inner landscape of a teacher's life.* San Francisco: Jossey-Bass.

Parker, L., & Shapiro, J. P. (1992). Where is the discussion of diversity in educational administration programs? Graduate students' voices addressing omission in their preparation. *Journal of School Leadership, 2*(1), 7–33.

Putnam, H. (1991). A reconsideration of Dewey and democracy. In M. Brint, & W. Weaver (Eds.), *Pragmatism in law and society.* Boulder, CO: Westview Press.

Robbins, B. (1993). *The phantom public sphere.* Minneapolis, MN: University of Minnesota Press.

Roseboro, D., & Gause, C. P. (2009). Faculty of color constructing communities at predominantly White institutions. In C. A. Mullen (Ed.), *Leadership and building professional learning communities* (pp. 139–150). New York: Palgrave Macmillan.

Rusch, E. (2004). Gender and race in leadership preparation: A constrained discourse. *Educational Administration Quarterly, 40*(1), 16–48.

Shields, C. M. (2004). Dialogic leadership for social justice: Overcoming pathologies of silence. *Educational Administration Quarterly, 40*(1), 109–132.

Skrla, L., Mckenzie, K. B., & Scheurich, J. (2009). *Using equity audits to create equitable and excellent schools.* California, CA: Corwin.

Somerville, S.B. (2000). *Queering the color line: Race the invention of homosexuality in American culture.* Durham, NC: Duke University Press.

Somerville, S. B. (2002). Queer fiction of race: Introduction. *MFS Modern Fiction Studies, 48*(4): 787–794.

Stanley, C. (2006). *Faculty of color: Teaching in predominantly white colleges and universities.* Massachusetts, MA: Anker.

Steinberg, S. (2001). *Multi/intercultural conversations: A reader.* New York: Peter Lang.

Steinberg, S. (2009). *Diversity and multiculturalism: A reader.* New York: Peter Lang.

Tate, W. F. (1994). From inner city to ivory tower: Does my voice matter in the academy? *Urban Education, 29*(3), 245–269.

Terry, J. (1999). *An American obsession: Science, medicine, and homosexuality in modern society.* Chicago: University of Chicago Press.

Thomas, G. (2001). The dual role of scholar and social change agent: Reflections from tenured African American and Latina faculty. In R.O. Maboleka & A. L. Green (Eds.), *Sisters of the academy: Emergent Black women scholars in higher education.* Sterling, VA: Stylus.

Weis, L. (1988). *Class, race, and gender in American education.* New York: State University Press.

Young, M. D., & Laible, J. (2000). White racism, antiracism, and school leadership preparation. *Journal of School Leadership, 10*, 374–415.

ABOUT THE AUTHOR

Dr. C. P. Gause is an Associate Professor in the Department of Teacher Education and Higher Education at The University of North Carolina-Greensboro. Over the past two years he has served as Co-chair of the Chancellor's Advisory Committee on Equity, Diversity and Inclusion. A former public school teacher, principal, and K-12 school administrator Gause received his Ph.D. in Educational Leadership from Miami University. He is co-editor of Keeping the Promise: Essays on Leadership, Democracy and Education (Peter Lang, 2007), this volume was a recipient of the 2007 American Educational Studies Association Critics Choice Award. His research interests include gender and queer studies; black masculinity; cultural studies; critical race theory; critical spirituality; and collaborative activism. He is author of Integration Matters: Navigating, Identity, Culture and Resistance (Peter Lang, 2008), which is a recipient of the 2009 American Educational Studies Association Critics Choice Award. This groundbreaking volume constructs a blueprint for realizing academic achievement and academic success for all students, particularly those who are members of under-represented populations. His third work, 201+ Strategies for Transforming Today's Schools (Booklocker.com, 2010); provides educators, administrators, teachers, parents, and students with practical tools, techniques, and strategies for effecting change in learning communities for the 21st century. His latest work, Diversity, Equity and Inclusive Education: A Voice from the Margins (Sense Publishers) moves the conversation of multiculturalism into the realm of critical diversity and inclusive education. This phenomenal text also continues Dr. Gause's crusade towards a seamless PreK-20 educational system; one that provides learners with a toolkit to engage in critical knowledge production, as well as critical knowledge consumption within a global context.

Contact Information:

C. P. Gause, PhD
Associate Professor
Teacher Education Higher Education
The University of North Carolina at Greensboro
Greensboro, NC 27405
cpgause@uncg.edu
drcpgause@gmail.com
www.drcpgause.com

CPSIA information can be obtained
at www.ICGtesting.com
Printed in the USA
FSOW04n2001220317
32235FS